The Supporters' Guide

to

Scottish Football

2004

EDITOR

John Robinson

Twelfth Edition

British Library Cataloguing in Publication Data
A catalogue record for this book is available from the British Library

ISBN 1-86223-075-7

Copyright © 2003, SOCCER BOOKS LIMITED (01472 696226)
72 St. Peter's Avenue, Cleethorpes, N.E. Lincolnshire, DN35 8HU, England
Web site   http://www.soccer-books.co.uk
e-mail   info@soccer-books.co.uk

Printed by The Cromwell Press

FOREWORD

We wish to thank the club secretaries of the Scottish Premier League, the Scottish League and the Highland League for their assistance in providing the information contained in this guide. We also wish to thank Bob Budd for the cover artwork and Tony Brown for providing the Cup Statistics.

When using this guide, readers should note that most clubs also extend the child concessionary prices to include Senior Citizens.

Additional copies of this guide can be obtained directly from us at the address shown on the facing page. Alternatively, orders may be placed securely via our web site – www.soccer-books.co.uk

Finally, we would like to wish our readers a happy and safe spectating season.

John Robinson
EDITOR

HAMPDEN – SCOTLAND'S NATIONAL STADIUM

Opened: 1903
Location: Hampden Park, Mount Florida, Glasgow G42 9BA
Telephone Nº: (0141) 620-4000
Fax Number: (0141) 620-4001

Record Attendance: 150,239
(Scotland vs England, 17th April 1937)
Pitch Size: 105 × 68 yards
Ground Capacity: 52,063 (All seats)
Web Site: www.hampdenpark.co.uk

GENERAL INFORMATION

Car Parking: *536 spaces + 39 disabled spaces at Stadium
Coach Parking: Stadium Coach Park
Nearest Railway Station: Mount Florida and King's Park (both are 5 minutes walk)
Nearest Bus Station: Buchanan Street
Nearest Police Station: Aikenhead Road, Glasgow
Police Telephone Nº: (0141) 532-4900

DISABLED INFORMATION

Wheelchairs: Accommodated in disabled spectators sections at all levels in the South Stand, particularly levels 1 and 4 where special catering and toilet facilities are available.
Disabled Toilets: Available
Commentaries are available for the blind
Contact: (0141) 620-4000

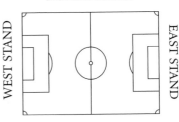

Travelling Supporters' Information:
Routes: From the South: Take the A724 to the Cambuslang Road and at Eastfield branch left into Main Street and follow through Burnhill Street and Westmuir Place into Prospecthill Road. Turn left into Aikenhead Road and right into Mount Annan for Kinghorn Drive and the Stadium; From the South: Take the A77 Fenwick Road, through Kilmarnock Road into Pollokshaws Road then turn right into Langside Avenue. Pass through Battle Place to Battlefield Road and turn left into Cathcart Road. Turn right into Letherby Drive, right into Carmunnock Road and 1st left into Mount Annan Drive for the Stadium; From the North & East: Exit M8 Junction 15 and passing Infirmary on left proceed into High Street and cross the Albert Bridge into Crown Street. Join Cathcart Road and proceed South until it becomes Carmunnock Road. Turn left into Mount Annan Drive and left again into Kinghorn Drive for the Stadium.

CONTENTS

THE SCOTTISH FOOTBALL ASSOCIATION

Founded 1873

Address National Stadium, Hampden Park, Mount Florida, Glasgow   G42 9BA

Web Site   www.scottishfa.co.uk

Phone   (0141) 616-6000

Fax   (0141) 616-6001

At the same address –

THE SCOTTISH FOOTBALL LEAGUE

Founded   1890

Phone   (0141) 620-4160

Fax   (0141) 620-4161

THE SCOTTISH PREMIER LEAGUE

Founded   1998

Web Site   www.scotprem.com

Phone   (0141) 620-4140

Fax   (0141) 620-4141

ABERDEEN FC

Founded: 1903 (**Entered League**: 1904)
Nickname: 'The Dons'
Ground: Pittodrie Stadium, Pittodrie Street, Aberdeen   AB24 5QH
Ground Capacity: 22,199 (all seats)
Record Attendance: 45,061 (13/3/54)
Pitch Size: 109 × 71 yards

Colours: Red shirts and shorts
Telephone N°: (01224) 650400
Ticket Office: (01224) 631903
Fax Number: (01224) 644173
Web Site: www.afc.co.uk

GENERAL INFORMATION

Car Parking: Beach Boulevard, King Street and Golf Road
Coach Parking: Beach Boulevard
Nearest Railway Station: Aberdeen (1 mile)
Nearest Bus Station: Aberdeen
Club Shop: At the ground and also Bridge Street, Aberdeen
Opening Times: 9.00am to 5.00pm
Telephone N°: (01224) 642800 or 212797
Police Telephone N°: (01224) 386000

GROUND INFORMATION

Away Supporters' Entrances & Sections:
Park Road entrance for the South Stand East

ADMISSION INFO (2003/2004 PRICES)

Adult Seating: £28.00
Child Seating: £2.00 to £20.00 (Under 12's)
Senior Citizen Seating/Under 18s: £5.00 to £20.00
Prices vary according to the category of the game
Programme Price: £2.50

DISABLED INFORMATION

Wheelchairs: Spaces available in the Merkland Stand
Helpers: One helper admitted per wheelchair
Prices: Free of charge for wheelchair-bound disabled. Helpers are charged concessionary prices
Disabled Toilets: One available in Richard Donald Stand and one is available by the Merkland Stand
Contact: (01224) 631903   (Bookings are necessary)

Travelling Supporters' Information:
Routes: From the City Centre, travel along Union Street then turn left into King Street. The Stadium is about ½ mile along King Street (A92) on the right-hand side.

AIRDRIE UNITED FC

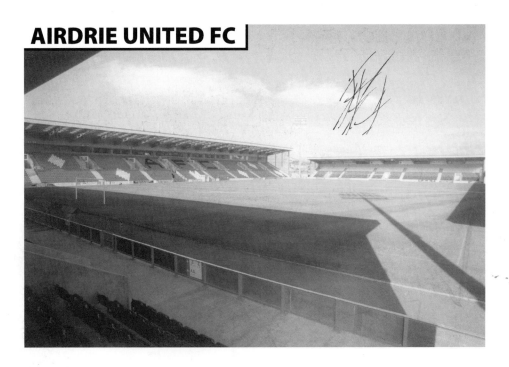

Founded: 1965 (**Entered League**: 1966)
Former Name: Clydebank FC
Ground: Excelsior Stadium, Broomfield Park, Craigneuk Avenue, Airdrie ML6 8QZ
Ground Capacity: 10,170 (All seats)
Record Attendance: 8,780 (1998/99)

Pitch Size: 115 × 71 yards
Colours: White shirts with Red diamond, White shorts
Telephone Nº: (07710) 230775
Ticket Office: (07710) 230775
Fax Number: (0141) 221-1497
Web Site: www.airdrieunitedfc.com

GENERAL INFORMATION

Car Parking: Behind all the Stands
Coach Parking: Behind the East Stand
Nearest Railway Station: Drumgelloch (½ mile – opens 3 hours before each match)
Nearest Bus Station: Gartlea – Airdrie Town Centre
Club Shop: At the ground
Opening Times: Opens 1 hour before matches
Telephone Nº: (07949) 976116
Police Telephone Nº: (01236) 762222

GROUND INFORMATION

Away Supporters' Entrances & Sections:
East and South Stands

ADMISSION INFO (2003/2004 PRICES)

Adult Seating: £12.00
Child Seating: £5.00
Programme Price: £1.50

DISABLED INFORMATION

Wheelchairs: Spaces available for home and away fans accommodated in the front sections
Helpers: One admitted per disabled supporter
Prices: Free for the disabled. Helpers half-price
Disabled Toilets: Available in all the stands
Contact: (01236) 622000   (Bookings are preferable)

Travelling Supporters' Information:
Routes: From the East: Exit the M8 at Junction 6 and take the A73 (signposted for Cumbernauld). Pass through Chapelhall into Airdrie and turn right into Petersburn Road – the ground is on the left; From the West: Take the A8 to the Chapelhall turn-off for Chapelhall. Join the A73 at Chapelhall, then as above.

ALBION ROVERS FC

Founded: 1882 (Entered League: 1903)
Nickname: 'Wee Rovers'
Ground: Cliftonhill Stadium, Main Street, Coatbridge, Lanarkshire ML5 3RB
Ground Capacity: 2,496
Seating Capacity: 538
Record Attendance: 27,381 (8/2/36)

Pitch Size: 110 × 72 yards
Colours: Yellow and Red shirts with Red shorts
Telephone Nº: (01236) 606334
Ticket Office: (01236) 607041
Fax Number: (01236) 606334
Web Site: www.albionrovers.com

GENERAL INFORMATION

Car Parking: Street parking and Albion Street
Coach Parking: Street parking only
Nearest Railway Station: Coatdyke (10 minutes walk)
Nearest Bus Station: Coatbridge
Club Shop: At the ground
Opening Times: One hour before each home match
Telephone Nº: (01236) 606334
Police Telephone Nº: –

GROUND INFORMATION

Away Supporters' Entrances & Sections:
Main Street entrance for the Main Street Area

ADMISSION INFO (2003/2004 PRICES)

Adult Standing: £8.00
Adult Seating: £8.00
Child Standing: £4.00
Child Seating: £4.00
Children under 12 are admitted free with a paying adult
Programme Price: £1.00

DISABLED INFORMATION

Wheelchairs: Approximately 30 spaces available in the Disabled Area
Helpers: Please phone the club for information
Prices: Please phone the club for information
Disabled Toilets: Available at the East End of the Ground
Contact: (01236) 606334 (Bookings are preferred)

Travelling Supporters' Information:
Routes: From the East or West: Take the A8/M8 to the Shawhead Interchange then follow the A725 to the Town Centre. Follow A89 signs towards Airdrie at the roundabout, the ground is then on the left; From the South: Take the A725 from Bellshill/Hamilton/Motherwell/M74 to Coatbridge. Follow the A89 signs towards Airdrie at the roundabout, the ground is then on the left; From the North: Take the A73 to Airdrie then follow signs for the A8010 to Coatbridge. Join the A89 and the ground is one mile on the right.

ALLOA ATHLETIC FC

Founded: 1878 (**Entered League**: 1921)
Nickname: 'The Wasps'
Ground: Recreation Park, Clackmannan Road, Alloa, FK10 1RY
Ground Capacity: 3,100
Seating Capacity: 400
Record Attendance: 13,000 (26/2/39)

Pitch Size: 110 × 75 yards
Colours: Gold and Black shirts with Black shorts
Telephone Nº: (01259) 722695
Ticket Office: (01259) 722695
Fax Number: (01259) 210886
Web Site: www.alloaathletic.co.uk

GENERAL INFORMATION

Car Parking: A Car Park is adjacent to the ground
Coach Parking: By Police Direction
Nearest Railway Station: Stirling (7 miles)
Nearest Bus Station: Alloa
Club Shop: At the ground
Opening Times: Matchdays only 1.30pm to 5.00pm
Telephone Nº: (01259) 722695
Police Telephone Nº: (01259) 723255

GROUND INFORMATION

Away Supporters' Entrances & Sections:
Hilton Road entrance for the Hilton Road Side and Clackmannan Road End

ADMISSION INFO (2003/2004 PRICES)

Adult Standing: £9.00
Adult Seating: £10.00
Senior Citizen/Child Standing: £5.00
Senior Citizen/Child Seating: £6.00
Programme Price: £1.50

DISABLED INFORMATION

Wheelchairs: Accommodated in the Disabled Section underneath the Main Stand
Helpers: Admitted
Prices: Free of charge for the disabled and helpers
Disabled Toilets: One available in the Main Stand
Contact: (01259) 722695   (Bookings are not necessary)

Travelling Supporters' Information:
Routes: From the South and East: Take the M74 to the M80 and exit at Junction 9 following the A907 into Alloa. Continue over two roundabouts passing the brewery and Town Centre. The Ground is on the left-hand side of the road.

ARBROATH FC

Founded: 1878 (**Entered League**: 1902)
Nickname: 'The Red Lichties'
Ground: Gayfield Park, Arbroath   DD11 1QB
Ground Capacity: 4,153
Seating Capacity: 848
Record Attendance: 13,510 (23/2/52)

Pitch Size: 115 × 70 yards
Colours: Maroon and White shirts with White shorts
Telephone Nº: (01241) 872157
Ticket Office: (01241) 872157
Fax Number: (01241) 431125
Web Site: www.arbroathfc.co.uk

GENERAL INFORMATION

Car Parking: Car Park in Queen's Drive
Coach Parking: Car Park in Queen's Drive
Nearest Railway Station: Arbroath (15 minutes walk)
Nearest Bus Station: Arbroath (10 minutes walk)
Club Shop: At the ground
Opening Times: Matchdays only 2.00pm – 5.00pm
Telephone Nº: (01241) 872838
Police Telephone Nº: (01241) 872222

GROUND INFORMATION

Away Supporters' Entrances & Sections:
Queen's Drive End

ADMISSION INFO (2003/2004 PRICES)

Adult Standing: £9.00
Adult Seating: £10.00
Concessionary Standing: £5.00
Concessionary Seating: £5.00
Family Ticket: 1 adult + 1 child £12.00
Programme Price: £1.20

DISABLED INFORMATION

Wheelchairs: 6 spaces available at both of the West and East Ends of the Main Stand
Helpers: Admitted
Prices: Normal prices for the disabled and helpers
Disabled Toilets: One available by the Club Shop
Contact: (01241) 872157   (Bookings are not necessary)

Travelling Supporters' Information:
Routes: From Dundee and the West: Take the A92 (Coast Road). On entering Arbroath, pass under the Railway Line and the ground is on the right-hand side; From Stonehaven/Montrose: Take the A92, pass through Arbroath, go past the Harbour and the ground is on the left-hand side.

AYR UNITED FC

Founded: 1910 (**Entered League**: 1910)
Former Names: Formed by the amagamation of Ayr Parkhouse FC and Ayr FC in 1910
Nickname: 'The Honest Men'
Ground: Somerset Park, Tryfield Place, Ayr, KA8 9NB
Ground Capacity: 10,185
Seating Capacity: 1,500

Record Attendance: 25,225 (13/9/69)
Pitch Size: 110 × 72 yards
Colours: White shirts and shorts
Telephone Nº: (01292) 263435/263436
Ticket Office: (01292) 263435/263436
Fax Number: (01292) 281314

GENERAL INFORMATION

Car Parking: Craigie Car Park, Ayr Racecourse and Somerset Road Car Park
Coach Parking: Craigie Car Park
Nearest Railway Station: Ayr or Newton-on-Ayr (both stations are 10 minutes walk)
Nearest Bus Station: Sandgate, Ayr
Club Shop: At the ground
Opening Times: Monday to Friday and Matchdays 8.30am to 5.30pm
Telephone Nº: (01292) 263435/263436
Police Telephone Nº: (01292) 664000

GROUND INFORMATION

Away Supporters' Entrances & Sections:
Turnstiles 1-7 for the Railway End (covered terrace) + turnstiles 9-10 for Main Stand accommodation

ADMISSION INFO (2003/2004 PRICES)

Adult Standing: £10.00
Adult Seating: £12.00 or £13.00
Child/Senior Citizen Standing: £5.00
Senior Citizen Seating: £7.00
Child Seating: In the Family Stand only – 1 Adult + 1 Child for £12.00 (each additional child is £5.00)
Programme Price: £1.70

DISABLED INFORMATION

Wheelchairs: 24 spaces are available in the Disabled Area beneath the Family Stand
Helpers: One admitted per wheelchair
Prices: Free for one wheelchair plus helper
Disabled Toilets: Available in the Disabled Area
Are Bookings Necessary: Only for all-ticket games
Contact: (01292) 263435/263436

Travelling Supporters' Information:
Routes: Make for the A77 Ring Road around Ayr, exit via Whitletts Roundabout onto the A719 and follow the road towards Ayr. Just past the end of the racecourse, turn right at the traffic lights into Burnett Terrace, a sharp left and then right takes you into Somerset Road for the ground. (For car parking on Matchdays turn left at the traffic lights and then right 50 yards on into Craigie Park or on Somerset Road just past the ground on the left into Somerset Road car park).

BERWICK RANGERS FC

Founded: 1881 (**Entered League**: 1951)
Nickname: 'The Borderers'
Ground: Shielfield Park, Shielfield Terrace, Tweedmouth, Berwick-upon-Tweed TD15 2EF
Ground Capacity: 4,131
Seating Capacity: 1,366
Record Attendance: 13,365 (28/1/67)

Pitch Size: 110 × 70 yards
Colours: Black and Gold striped shirts, Black shorts
Telephone Nº: (01289) 307424
Ticket Office: (01289) 307424
Fax Number: (01289) 309424
Independent Web Site: www.theducket.com

GENERAL INFORMATION

Car Parking: Large Car Park at the ground
Coach Parking: Car Park at the ground
Nearest Railway Station: Berwick-upon-Tweed (1½ miles)
Nearest Bus Station: Berwick Town Centre (1 mile)
Club Shop: At the Supporters' Club in the ground
Opening Times: Matchdays Only
Telephone Nº: (01289) 307424
Police Telephone Nº: (01289) 307111

GROUND INFORMATION

Away Supporters' Entrances & Sections:
Shielfield Terrace entrance for the Popular Side Terrace (Gates A or B), Gate B for Main Stand accommodation

ADMISSION INFO (2003/2004 PRICES)

Adult Standing: £9.00
Adult Seating: £9.00
Concessions: £4.00
Under 13s are admitted for £1.00 when with a paying adult
Programme Price: £1.50

DISABLED INFORMATION

Wheelchairs: Accommodated in the Main Stand
Helpers: Admitted with wheelchair disabled
Prices: The disabled are admitted free of charge
Disabled Toilets: Available in the General Toilet Block and also in the Club Offices
Contact: (01289) 307424/307623 (Bookings are necessary)

Travelling Supporters' Information:
Routes: From the North: Take the A1 (Berwick Bypass), cross the new road-bridge then take the 1st exit at the roundabout. Carry on for approximately ¼ mile to the next roundabout, go straight across then continue for approximately ¼ mile into Shielfield Terrace. Turn left and the ground is on the left; From the South: Take the A1 Bypass and continue across the first roundabout signposted Scremerston/Tweedmouth and then on for 1 mile. At the crossroads/junction take 'Spittal' Road (right) and continue for approximately 1 mile until the road becomes Shielfield Terrace. The ground is on the left in Shielfield Terrace.

BRECHIN CITY FC

Founded: 1906 (**Entered League**: 1923)
Nickname: 'The City'
Ground: Glebe Park, Trinity Road, Brechin, Angus, DD9 6BJ
Ground Capacity: 3,960
Seating Capacity: 1,519
Record Attendance: 8,244 (3/2/73)

Pitch Size: 110 × 67 yards
Colours: Red and White shirts and shorts
Telephone Nº: (01356) 622856
Ticket Office: (01356) 622856
Fax Number: (01356) 625667
Secretary's Number: (01356) 625691
Web Site: www.brechincity.co.uk

GENERAL INFORMATION
Car Parking: Small Car Park at the ground and street parking
Coach Parking: Street parking
Nearest Railway Station: Montrose (8 miles)
Nearest Bus Station: Brechin
Club Shop: At the ground
Opening Times: Matchdays Only
Telephone Nº: (01356) 622856
Police Telephone Nº: (01356) 622222

GROUND INFORMATION
Away Supporters' Entrances & Sections:
No segregation usually

ADMISSION INFO (2003/2004 PRICES)
Adult Standing: £7.00
Adult Seating: £8.00
Child Standing: £3.00
Child Seating: £3.00
Programme Price: £1.00

DISABLED INFORMATION
Wheelchairs: 10 spaces each for home and away fans
Helpers: Please phone the club for details
Prices: Please phone the club for details
Disabled Toilets: Two are available in the Covered Enclosure
Contact: (01356) 622856   (Bookings are not necessary)

Travelling Supporters' Information:
Routes: From the South and West: Take the M90 to the A94 and continue along past the first 'Brechin' turn-off. Take the second turn signposted 'Brechin'. On entering Brechin, the ground is on the left-hand side of the road between some houses.

CELTIC FC

Founded: 1888 (**Entered League**: 1890)
Nickname: 'The Bhoys' 'The Hoops'
Ground: Celtic Park, Glasgow   G40 3RE
Ground Capacity: 60,355 (All seats)
Record Attendance: 92,000 (1/1/38)
Pitch Size: 115 × 74 yards

Colours: Green & White hooped shirts, White shorts
Telephone Nº: (0141) 556-2611
Ticket Office: (0141) 551-8653
Fax Number: (0141) 551-8106
Web Site: www.celticfc.co.uk

GENERAL INFORMATION

Car Parking: Limited on Matchdays to those with a Valid Car Park Pass. Otherwise, street parking
Coach Parking: Gallowgate, Fielden Street, Biggar Street and Nuneaton Street
Nearest Railway Station: Bellgrove (10 minutes walk)
Nearest Bus Stop: Outside of the ground
Club Shop: Superstore at Celtic Park. Also: 21 High Street, Glasgow; 40 Dundas St., Glasgow; 154 Argyle St., Glasgow; 34 Frederick St., Edinburgh and Level 1, Jervis Centre, Dublin
Opening Times: Superstore: Mon-Sat 9am-6pm. Sundays 10am-5pm; North Stand: 2 hours before kick-off & half-time; High Street: Mon-Sat 9.30-5.30, Sunday 11.30-4.30; Dundas Street: Mon-Sat 9-5; Dublin Shop: Mon-Sat at least 9.30-6.00 (later on some days). Also Sundays 12.00pm–6.00pm
Telephone Nº: (0141) 554-4231 (Superstore)
Police Telephone Nº: (0141) 532-4600

GROUND INFORMATION

Away Supporters' Entrances & Sections:
Kinloch Street Turnstiles for the East Stand

ADMISSION INFO (2003/2004 PRICES)

Adult Seating: £20.00 – £24.00
Child Seating: £12.00 – £14.00
Programme Price: £2.00

DISABLED INFORMATION

Wheelchairs: 141 spaces for home fans and 6 spaces for away fans in the North Stand and East Stand
Helpers: 144 helpers admitted in total
Prices: £3.00 – £5.00 subject to availability (there is a waiting list). This covers a disabled fan and a helper
Disabled Toilets: 5 available in the North Stand, 2 in the East Stand and 3 in the South West Stand
Contact: (0141) 551-4311   (Bookings are necessary)

Travelling Supporters' Information:
Routes: From the South and East: Take the A74 London Road towards the City Centre, Celtic Park is on the right about ½ mile past the Belvidere Hospital and the ground is clearly visible; From the West: Take the A74 London Road from the City Centre and turn left about ½ mile past Bridgeton Station.

CLYDE FC

Founded: 1877 (**Entered League**: 1906)
Nickname: 'Bully Wee'
Ground: Broadwood Stadium, Cumbenauld, Glasgow G68 9NE
Ground Capacity: 8,200 (all seats)
Record Attendance: 8,000 (14/8/96)
Pitch Size: 115 × 75 yards

Colours: Shirts are White with Black piping, Shorts are Black
Telephone Nº: (01236) 451511
Ticket Office: (01236) 451511
Fax Number: (01236) 733490
Web Site: www.clydefc.co.uk

GENERAL INFORMATION

Car Parking: Behind the Main and West Stands
Coach Parking: Behind the Main Stand
Nearest Railway Station: Croy (1½ miles)
Nearest Bus Station: Cumbernauld Town Centre
Club Shop: At the ground
Opening Times: One hour before and after the match
Telephone Nº: (01236) 451511
Police Telephone Nº: (01236) 736085

GROUND INFORMATION

Away Supporters' Entrances & Sections:
West Stand Turnstile for the West Stand area

ADMISSION INFO (2003/2004 PRICES)

Adult Seating: £13.00
Child Seating: £6.00
Concessionary Seating: £6.00
Programme Price: £2.00

DISABLED INFORMATION

Wheelchairs: 10 spaces each for home and away fans accommodated in front sections of each stand
Helpers: One helper admitted per wheelchair
Prices: Free of charge for the disabled
Disabled Toilets: 4 available in the Main and West Stands
Contact: (01236) 451511 (Bookings are not necessary)

Travelling Supporters' Information:
Routes: From all Parts: Exit the A80 at Broadwood Junction and follow the signs for Broadwood. The ground is signposted from the next roundabout.

COWDENBEATH FC

Founded: 1881 (**Entered League**: 1905)
Nickname: 'Cowden' 'Blue Brazil'
Ground: Central Park, High Street, Cowdenbeath KY4 9QQ
Ground Capacity: 4,370
Seating Capacity: 1,431
Record Attendance: 25,586 (21/9/49)
Pitch Size: 107 × 64 yards

Colours: Shirts are Royal Blue with White trim, Shorts are White
Telephone Nº: (01383) 610166
Ticket Office: (01383) 610166
Fax Number: (01383) 512132
Web Site: www.cowdenbeathfc.com

GENERAL INFORMATION

Car Parking: Car Park at the ground and Stenhouse Street (200 yards). A total of 200 spaces are available
Coach Parking: King Street and Rowan Terrace
Nearest Railway Station: Cowdenbeath (400 yards)
Nearest Bus Station: Cowdenbeath (Bus Stop at ground)
Club Shop: At the ground
Opening Times: Weekdays 10.00am to 3.00pm; Saturdays 1.00pm to 3.00pm
Telephone Nº: (01383) 610166
Police Telephone Nº: (01383) 318600

GROUND INFORMATION

Away Supporters' Entrances & Sections:
Main Entrance for the South and East Sides

ADMISSION INFO (2003/2004 PRICES)

Adult Standing: £8.00
Adult Seating: £9.00
Child Standing: £3.00
Child Seating: £3.50
Programme Price: £1.00

DISABLED INFORMATION

Wheelchairs: 3 spaces each for home and away fans
Helpers: Please phone the club for information
Prices: Please phone the club for information
Disabled Toilets: 1 Ladies, 1 Gents and 1 Unisex available
Contact: (01383) 610166 (Bookings are necessary)

Travelling Supporters' Information:
Routes: Exit the M90 at Junction 3 for Dunfermline. Take the Dual Carriageway to Cowdenbeath and follow straight on into the High Street. The ground is situated on the first left turn in the High Street.

DUMBARTON FC

Founded: 1872 (**Entered League**: 1890)
Nickname: 'Sons'
Ground: Strathclyde Homes Stadium, Castle Road, Dumbarton G82 1JJ
Ground Capacity: 2,046 (All seats)
Record Attendance: 2,035 (27th January 2001)

Pitch Size: 110 × 72 yards
Colours: Shirts are Gold with Black Trim, Black shorts
Telephone Nº: (01389) 762569
Ticket Office: (01389) 762569
Fax Number: (01389) 762629
Web Site: www.dumbartonfootballclub.com

GENERAL INFORMATION

Car Parking: 400 spaces available at the ground
Coach Parking: At the ground
Nearest Railway Station: Dumbarton East
Nearest Bus Station: Dumbarton
Club Shop: At the ground
Opening Times: Weekdays and Saturday matchdays 10.00am to 4.00pm
Telephone Nº: (01389) 762569
Police Telephone Nº: (01389) 822000

GROUND INFORMATION

Away Supporters' Entrances & Sections:
West Section

ADMISSION INFO (2003/2004 PRICES)

Adult Seating: £10.00
Child Seating: £5.00
Programme Price: £1.00

DISABLED INFORMATION

Wheelchairs: Approximately 24 spaces available in the disabled area
Helpers: Please phone the club for information
Prices: Please phone the club for information
Disabled Toilets: Available
Contact: (01389) 762569 (Bookings are necessary)

Travelling Supporters' Information:
Routes: The ground is situated just by Dumbarton Castle. Take the A814 into Dumbarton and follow the brown signs for the Castle to find the ground.

DUNDEE FC

Founded: 1893 (**Entered League**: 1893)
Nickname: 'The Dee'
Ground: Dens Park Stadium, Sandeman Street, Dundee   DD3 7JY
Ground Capacity: 11,850 (All seats)
Record Attendance: 43,024 (7/2/53)

Pitch Size: 105 × 70 yards
Colours: Blue shirts with White shorts
Telephone Nº: (01382) 889966
Ticket Office: (01382) 889966
Fax Number: (01382) 832284
Web Site: www.dundeefc.co.uk

GENERAL INFORMATION

Car Parking: Private 600 space Car Park available
Coach Parking: 50 yards from the ground
Nearest Railway Station: Dundee
Nearest Bus Station: Dundee
Club Shop: Commercial Street, Dundee
Opening Times: Weekdays from 10.00am to 5.00pm
Telephone Nº: (01382) 889966
Police Telephone Nº: (01382) 223200

GROUND INFORMATION

Away Supporters' Entrances & Sections:
Turnstiles 33-38 for East Stand accommodation

ADMISSION INFO (2003/2004 PRICES)

Adult Seating: £12.00 – £20.00
Child Seating: £4.00 – £12.00
Reduced prices for children are available in the Family Stand
Senior Citizen Seating: £8.00 – £12.00
Programme Price: £2.00

DISABLED INFORMATION

Wheelchairs: Accommodated in the East and West Stands
Helpers: Admitted
Prices: Free for the disabled. £12.00 – £14.00 for helpers
Disabled Toilets: Adjacent to the Disabled Area
Contact: (01382) 889966   (Bookings are necessary)

Travelling Supporters' Information:
Routes: Take the A972 from Perth (Kingsway West) to King's Cross Circus Roundabout. Take the 3rd exit into Clepington Road and turn right into Provost Road for 1 mile then take the 2nd left into Sandeman Street for the ground.

DUNDEE UNITED FC

Founded: 1909 (**Entered League**: 1910)
Former Names: Dundee Hibernians FC
Nickname: 'The Terrors'
Ground: Tannadice Park, Tannadice Street, Dundee, DD3 7JW
Ground Capacity: 14,223 (all seats)
Record Attendance: 28,000 (November 1966)

Pitch Size: 110 × 72 yards
Colours: Tangerine shirts and shorts
Telephone Nº: (01382) 833166
Ticket Office: (01382) 833166
Fax Number: (01382) 889398
Web Site: www.dundeeunitedfc.co.uk

GENERAL INFORMATION

Car Parking: Street Parking and Melrose Car Park
Coach Parking: Gussie Park (home coaches) and Dens Field (away coaches)
Nearest Railway Station: Dundee (20 minutes walk)
Nearest Bus Station: Dundee
Club Shop: At the ground on Matchdays only or at 5 Victoria Road, Dundee DD1 1ER
Opening Times: At the ground: Matchdays from 2.00pm to 5.00pm; Victoria Road: Monday – Saturday 9.00am–5.30pm
Telephone Nº: (01382) 204066
Police Telephone Nº: (01382) 223200

GROUND INFORMATION

Away Supporters' Entrances & Sections:
Turnstiles 7-16 for South Stand & Fair Play Stand

ADMISSION INFO (2003/2004 PRICES)

Adult Seating: £16.00 – £20.00
Child Seating: £9.00 – £11.00
Programme Price: £2.00

DISABLED INFORMATION

Wheelchairs: Accommodated in the George Fox Stand and the East and West Stands
Helpers: Please phone the club for details
Prices: Please phone the club for details
Disabled Toilets: Available in the George Fox Stand and in the East and West Stands
Contact: (01382) 833166   (Bookings are necessary)

Travelling Supporters' Information:
Routes: From the South or West: Travel via Perth and take the A90 to Dundee. Once in Dundee join the Kingsway (ring road) and follow until the third roundabout then turn right onto Old Glamis Road. Follow the road to join Provost Road then turn left into Sandeman Street for the ground; From the North: Follow the A90 from Aberdeen and join the Kingsway (ring road). At the first set of traffic lights turn right into Clepington Road and follow into Arklay Street before turning right into Tannadice Street for the ground.

DUNFERMLINE ATHLETIC FC

Founded: 1885 (**Entered League**: 1921)
Nickname: 'The Pars'
Ground: East End Park, Halbeath Road, Dunfermline, Fife, KY12 7RB
Ground Capacity: 12,558 (All seats)
Record Attendance: 27,816 (30/4/68)

Pitch Size: 115 × 70 yards
Colours: Black and White striped shirts, White shorts
Telephone Nº: (01383) 724295
Ticket Office: (0870) 300-1201
Fax Number: (01383) 723468
Web Site: www.dafc.co.uk
Club Call Nº: (01383) 724295

GENERAL INFORMATION

Car Parking: Street Parking and a Car Park at the ground. Also, a Multistorey Car Park is 10 minutes walk
Coach Parking: Leys Park Road
Nearest Railway Station: Dunfermline (15 minutes walk)
Nearest Bus Station: Carnegie Drive, Dunfermline (10 minutes walk)
Club Shop: Kingsgate Shopping Centre, Dunfermline
Opening Times: Monday to Saturday 9.00am – 5.00pm
Telephone Nº: (01383) 626737
Police Telephone Nº: (01383) 726711

GROUND INFORMATION

Away Supporters' Entrances & Sections:
Turnstiles 10-15 for the East Stand. Turnstiles 16-18 for the North East Stand

ADMISSION INFO (2003/2004 PRICES)

Adult Seating: £12.00 – £18.00
Child Seating: £6.00 – £13.00
Note: Match prices vary according to the category of game
Programme Price: £2.00

DISABLED INFORMATION

Wheelchairs: 12 spaces each for home & away fans
Helpers: One admitted per wheelchair
Prices: Free for each wheelchair disabled and helper
Disabled Toilets: Available in West and East Stands
Contact: (01383) 726863   (Bookings are necessary)

Travelling Supporters' Information:
Routes: From the Forth Road Bridge and Perth: Exit the M90 at Junction 3 and take the A907 (Halbeath Road) into Dunfermline – the ground is on right; From Kincardine Bridge and Alloa: Take the A985 to the A994 into Dunfermline. Take Pittencrief Street, Glen Bridge and Carnegie Drive to Sinclair Gardens roundabout. Take the 1st exit toward the Traffic Lights then turn right into Ley's Park Road. Take the second exit on the right into the Car Park at the rear of the stadium.

EAST FIFE FC

Founded: 1903 (**Entered League**: 1903)
Nickname: 'The Fifers'
Ground: Bayview Stadium, Harbour View, Methil,
Fife   KY8 3RW
Ground Capacity: 2,000 (All seats)
Record Attendance: 22,515 (2/1/50)

Pitch Size: 113 × 73 yards
Colours: Black and Gold striped shirts, White shorts
Telephone N°: (01333) 426323
Ticket Office: (01333) 426323
Fax Number: (01333) 426376
Web Site: www.eastfife.org

GENERAL INFORMATION

Car Parking: Adjacent to the ground
Coach Parking: Adjacent to the ground
Nearest Railway Station: Kirkcaldy (8 miles)
Nearest Bus Station: Leven
Club Shop: At the ground
Opening Times: Matchdays and normal office hours
Telephone N°: (01333) 426323
Police Telephone N°: (01592) 418900

GROUND INFORMATION

Away Supporters' Entrances & Sections:
Accommodated within the Main Stand

ADMISSION INFO (2003/2004 PRICES)

Adult Seating: £10.00
Child Seating: £5.00
Programme Price: £1.00

DISABLED INFORMATION

Wheelchairs: 24 spaces available in total
Helpers: Admitted
Prices: Normal prices charged
Disabled Toilets: Yes
Contact: (01333) 426323   (Bookings are necessary)

Travelling Supporters' Information:
Routes: Take the A915 from Kirkcaldy past Buckhaven and Methil to Leven. Turn right at the traffic lights and go straight on at the first roundabout then turn right at the second roundabout. Cross Bawbee Bridge and turn left at the next roundabout. The ground is the first turning on the left after ¼ mile.

EAST STIRLINGSHIRE FC

Founded: 1881 (**Entered League**: 1900)
Former Names: Bainsford Britannia FC
Nickname: 'The Shire'
Ground: Firs Park, Firs Street, Falkirk   FK2 7AY
Ground Capacity: 780
Seating Capacity: 280
Record Attendance: 12,000 (21/2/21)

Pitch Size: 112 × 72 yards
Colours: Shirts are Black with White hoops, Black shorts
Telephone Nº: (01324) 623583
Ticket Office: (01324) 623583
Fax Number: (01324) 637862
Web Site: None

GENERAL INFORMATION
Car Parking: Street parking
Coach Parking: Street parking
Nearest Railway Station: Grahamston (10 minutes walk)
Nearest Bus Station: Falkirk
Club Shop: At the ground
Opening Times: Weekdays (except Wednesdays) and
Saturday Matchdays 10.00am to 12.00pm
Telephone Nº: (01324) 623583
Police Telephone Nº: (01324) 634212

GROUND INFORMATION
Away Supporters' Entrances & Sections:
No usual segregation

ADMISSION INFO (2003/2004 PRICES)
Adult Standing: £8.00
Adult Seating: £10.00
OAP and Child Standing: £4.00
OAP and Child Seating: £6.00
Programme Price: £1.00

DISABLED INFORMATION
Wheelchairs: Accommodated
Helpers: Admitted
Prices: £4.00 each for both disabled and helpers
Disabled Toilets: Available in the Main Stand
Contact: (01324) 623583   (Bookings are necessary)

Travelling Supporters' Information:
Routes: From Glasgow and Edinburgh: Exit the Motorway at signs marked Grangemouth. Follow the AA signs for football traffic into Falkirk as far as Thornhill Road (where the road meets the 'Give Way' sign). Once in Thornhill Road turn left into Firs Street at St. James' Church. The ground is straight ahead.

ELGIN CITY FC

Founded: 1893   (**Entered League**: 2000)
Nickname: 'Black and Whites'
Ground: Borough Briggs, Borough Briggs Road, Elgin   IV30 1AP
Ground Capacity: 3,900
Seating Capacity: 478
Record Attendance: 12,640 (17/2/68)

Pitch Size: 120 × 86 yards
Colours: Black and White shirts with Black shorts
Telephone Nº: (01343) 551114
Ticket Information: (01343) 551114
Fax Number: (01343) 547921
Web Site: www.elgincity.com (Unofficial site)

GENERAL INFORMATION
Car Parking: At the ground
Coach Parking: At the ground
Nearest Railway Station: Elgin (1 mile)
Nearest Bus Station: Elgin (¼ mile)
Club Shop: At the ground
Opening Times: Weekdays 9.30am to 5.30pm and also Saturdays 9.30am to 3.00pm
Telephone Nº: (01343) 551114
Police Telephone Nº: (01343) 543101

GROUND INFORMATION
Away Supporters' Entrances & Sections:
West End entrances for the Covered Enclosure

ADMISSION INFO (2003/2004 PRICES)
Adult Standing: £7.00
Adult Seating: £9.00
Child Standing: £3.50
Child Seating: £5.00
Programme Price: £1.00

DISABLED INFORMATION
Wheelchairs: Accommodated
Helpers: Admitted
Prices: The disabled are admitted at concessionary prices
Disabled Toilets: Available
Contact: (01343) 551114   (Bookings are not necessary)

Travelling Supporters' Information:
Routes: Take the Alexandra bypass to the roundabout ½ mile from the City Centre and turn left towards Lossiemouth. Borough Briggs Road is on the left.

FALKIRK FC

Falkirk FC are groundsharing with Stenhousemuir FC for the 2003/2004 season while their new ground is under construction.

Founded: 1876 (**Entered League**: 1902)
Nickname: 'The Bairns'
Office Address: Grangemouth Enterprise Centre, Falkirk Road, Grangemouth FK3 8XF
Record Attendance: 12,500 (11th March 1950)
Pitch Size: 110 x 72 yards

Colours: Navy Blue shirts with White shorts
Telephone N°: (01324) 666808
Ticket Office: (01324) 666808
Fax Number: (01324) 664539
Web Site: www.falkirkfc.co.uk

GENERAL INFORMATION

Car Parking: A Large Car Park is adjacent
Coach Parking: Behind the North Terracing
Nearest Railway Station: Larbert (1 mile)
Nearest Bus Station: Falkirk (2½ miles)
Club Shop: Glebe Street, Falkirk
Opening Times: 9.00am to 5.00pm
Telephone N°: (01324) 639366
Police Telephone N°: (01324) 562112

GROUND INFORMATION

Away Supporters' Entrances & Sections:
Terracing entrances and accommodation

ADMISSION INFO (2003/2004 PRICES)

Adult Standing: £12.00
Adult Seating: £14.00 – £17.00
Child Standing: £6.00 (£2.00 for Under-11's)
Child Seating: £7.00 – £13.50
Programme Price: £1.50

DISABLED INFORMATION

Wheelchairs: Accommodated
Helpers: Admitted
Prices: Normal prices are charged
Disabled Toilets: Available in the Gladstone Road Stand
Contact: (01324) 66808 (Bookings are necessary)

Travelling Supporters' Information:
Routes: Exit the M876 at Junction 2 and follow signs for Stenhousemuir. Pass the Old Hospital and turn right after the Golf Course. The ground is on the left behind the houses – the floodlights are visible for ¼ mile.

FORFAR ATHLETIC FC

Founded: 1885 (**Entered League**: 1921)
Nickname: 'Loons'
Ground: Station Park, Carseview Road, Forfar, Angus
Ground Capacity: 4,602
Seating Capacity: 739
Record Attendance: 10,780 (2/2/70)

Pitch Size: 115 × 69 yards
Colours: Sky Blue shirts with Navy trim, Navy shorts
Telephone Nº: (01307) 463576
Ticket Office: (01307) 463576
Fax Number: (01307) 466956
Web Site: www.forfarathletic.co.uk

GENERAL INFORMATION
Car Parking: Market Muir Car Park and adjacent streets
Coach Parking: Market Muir Car Park
Nearest Railway Station: Dundee or Arbroath (14 miles)
Nearest Bus Station: Forfar (½ mile)
Club Shop: None
Police Telephone Nº: (01307) 462551

GROUND INFORMATION
Away Supporters' Entrances & Sections:
West End entrances for West End Terracing and North part of the Main Stand

ADMISSION INFO (2003/2004 PRICES)
Adult Standing: £9.00
Adult Seating: £9.50
Child Standing: £4.00
Child Seating: £4.50
Programme Price: £1.00

DISABLED INFORMATION
Wheelchairs: 4 spaces each for home and away fans accommodated to the west of the Main Stand
Helpers: Please phone the club for details
Prices: Please phone the club for details
Disabled Toilets: One available
Contact: (01307) 463576 (Bookings are necessary)

Travelling Supporters' Information:
Routes: Take the A85/M90 to Dundee and then the A929. Exit at the 2nd turn-off (signposted for Forfar). On the outskirts of Forfar, turn right at the T-junction and then left at the next major road. The ground is signposted on the left (down the cobbled street with the railway arch).

GREENOCK MORTON FC

Founded: 1874 (**Entered League**: 1893)
Nickname: 'Ton'
Ground: Cappielow Park, Sinclair Street, Greenock, PA15 2TY
Ground Capacity: 14,267
Seating Capacity: 5,257
Record Attendance: 23,500 (29/4/21)

Pitch Size: 110 × 71 yards
Colours: Blue and White hooped shirts, White shorts
Telephone Nº: (01475) 723571
Ticket Office: (01475) 723571
Fax Number: (01475) 781084
Web Site: www.gmfc.net

GENERAL INFORMATION

Car Parking: At the ground
Coach Parking: James Watt Dock
Nearest Railway Station: Cartsdyke (½ mile)
Nearest Bus Station: Town Centre (1½ miles)
Club Shop: At the ground
Opening Times: Weekdays 10.00am to 4.00pm. Saturday matchdays open before and after the match
Telephone Nº: (01475) 723571 **Fax Nº**: (01475) 728771
Police Telephone Nº: (01475) 724444

GROUND INFORMATION

Away Supporters' Entrances & Sections:
East Hamilton Street turnstiles

ADMISSION INFO (2003/2004 PRICES)

Adult Standing: £9.00
Adult Seating: £11.00
Child Standing: £2.00
Parent & Child Seating: £14.00
Senior Citizen Standing: £5.00
Senior Citizen Seating: £6.00
Programme Price: £1.50

DISABLED INFORMATION

Wheelchairs: 5 spaces each for home and away fans accommodated below the Grandstand
Helpers: One helper admitted per disabled fan
Prices: Free of charge for the disabled and helpers
Disabled Toilets: One available
Contact: (01475) 723571 (Bookings are necessary)

Travelling Supporters' Information:
Routes: From All Parts: Take the M8 to the A8. Pass through Port Glasgow and turn left after passing the dockyard buildings on the right-hand side of the road.

GRETNA FC

Founded: 1946 (**Entered League**: 2002)
Nickname: 'Black and Whites'
Ground: Raydale Park, Dominion Road, Gretna, DG16 5AP
Ground Capacity: 2,200
Seating Capacity: 385

Record Attendance: 2,307 (1991)
Pitch Size: 110 × 70 yards
Colours: Black and White hooped shirts, Black shorts
Telephone Nº: (01461) 337602
Fax Number: (01461) 338047
Web Site: www.gretnafootballclub.co.uk

GENERAL INFORMATION
Car Parking: At the ground
Coach Parking: At the ground
Nearest Railway Station: Gretna Green
Nearest Bus Station: Carlisle
Club Shop: At the ground
Opening Times: Monday to Saturday 10.00am to 5.00pm
Telephone Nº: (01461) 337602
Police Telephone Nº: (01461) 338345

GROUND INFORMATION
Away Supporters' Entrances & Sections:
West Enclosure

ADMISSION INFO (2003/2004 PRICES)
Adult Standing: £7.00
Adult Seating: £8.00
Child Standing: £3.50
Child Seating: £4.00
Programme Price: £1.50

DISABLED INFORMATION
Wheelchairs: Not accommodated at present but please call for details of developments
Disabled Toilets: Yes
Contact: (01461) 337602

Travelling Supporters' Information:
Routes: From All Parts: Leave the A74 at the Gretna turn-off and exit onto the B7076. Cross Border Bridge with the Gretna Chase Hotel on the right then turn left at the Crossways Inn into Annan Road. After ¼ mile turn left into Dominion Road and the ground is on the right.

HAMILTON ACADEMICAL FC

Founded: 1874 (**Entered League**: 1897)
Nickname: 'The Accies'
Ground: New Douglas Park, Cadzow Avenue, Hamilton ML3 0FT
Ground Capacity: 5,406 (all seats)
Record Attendance: 28,690 (at the Old Ground)

Pitch Size: 115 × 75 yards
Colours: Red and White hooped shirts, shorts are White with a Red flash
Telephone Nº: (01698) 368650
Fax Number: (01698) 285422
Web Site: None

GENERAL INFORMATION
Car Parking: At the ground and adjacent Council Car Park
Coach Parking: By Police Direction
Nearest Railway Station: Hamilton West (200 yards)
Nearest Bus Station: Hamilton (1 mile)
Club Shop: At the Stadium
Opening Times: Office hours only
Telephone Nº: (01698) 368650
Police Telephone Nº: (01698) 483300

GROUND INFORMATION
Away Supporters' Entrances & Sections:
North Stand – use turnstiles 10, 11 & 12

ADMISSION INFO (2003/2004 PRICES)
Adult Seating: £10.00
Child/Senior Citizen Seating: £5.00
Programme Price: £2.00

DISABLED INFORMATION
Wheelchairs: Accommodated in the front row of the stand or by the trackside
Helpers: Admitted following prior booking
Prices: Free for the disabled and one helper
Disabled Toilets: Available
Contact: (01698) 368650 (Bookings are necessary)

Travelling Supporters' Information:
Routes: Exit the M74 at Junction 5 and follow signs marked "Football Traffic". Go past Hamilton Racecourse, turn right at the lights then first right again for New Park Street and Auchinraith Avenue for the ground.

HEART OF MIDLOTHIAN FC

Founded: 1874 (**Entered League**: 1890)
Nickname: 'The Jam Tarts' 'Jambos'
Ground: Tynecastle Stadium, Gorgie Road,
Edinburgh   EH11 2NL
Ground Capacity: 18,000 (All seats)
Record Attendance: 53,496 (13/1/32)
Pitch Size: 107 × 73 yards

Colours: Maroon shirts with White shorts
Telephone N°: (0131) 200-7200
Ticket Office: (0131) 200-7201
Fax Number: (0131) 200-7222
Web Site: www.heartsfc.co.uk

GENERAL INFORMATION

Car Parking: Street Parking in Robertson Avenue and Westfield Road
Coach Parking: Russell Road
Nearest Railway Station: Edinburgh Haymarket (½ mile)
Nearest Bus Station: St. Andrew's Square
Club Superstore: Gorgie Stand/Tynecastle Terrace
Opening Times: Weekdays 9.30am to 5.30pm and Matchdays 9.30am to 5.00pm
Telephone N°: (0131) 200-7211
Police Telephone N°: (0131) 229-2323

GROUND INFORMATION

Away Supporters' Entrances & Sections:
Roseburn Stand entrances and accommodation

ADMISSION INFO (2003/2004 PRICES)

Adult Seating: £15.00 – £20.00
Child Seating: £10.00 (In the Family Area only)
Note: Prices vary depending on the category of the game
Programme: £2.00

DISABLED INFORMATION

Wheelchairs: 100 spaces available for home and away fans in Wheatfield, Roseburn & Gorgie Stands
Helpers: Admitted
Prices: £10.00
Disabled Toilets: Available
Contact: (0131) 200-7201   (Bookings are necessary)

Travelling Supporters' Information:
Routes: From the West: Take the A71 (Ayr Road) into Gorgie Road and the ground is about ¾ mile past Saughton Park on the left; From the North: Take the A90 Queensferry Road and turn right into Drum Brae after about ½ mile. Follow Drum Brae into Meadowplace Road (about 1 mile) then Broomhouse Road to the junction with Calder Road. Turn right, then as from the West;   From the South: Take the A702/A703 to the A720 (Oxgangs Road). Turn left and follow the A720 into Wester Hailes Road (2½ miles) until the junction with Calder Road. Turn right, then as from the West.

HIBERNIAN FC

Founded: 1875 (**Entered League**: 1893)
Nickname: 'The Hi-Bees'
Ground: Easter Road Stadium, 12 Albion Place,
Edinburgh   EH7 5QG
Ground Capacity: 17,462 (all seats)
Record Attendance: 65,840 (2/1/50)
Pitch Size: 115 × 70 yards

Colours: Green and White shirts with White shorts
Telephone Nº: (0131) 661-2159
Ticket Office: (0131) 661-1875
24-hour Ticket Hotline: (0870) 840-1875
Fax Number: (0131) 659-6488
Web Site: www.hibernianfc.co.uk
Info Line Nº: (0131) 661-1875

GENERAL INFORMATION

Car Parking: Street parking
Coach Parking: Regent Road (by Police Direction)
Nearest Railway Station: Edinburgh Waverley
(25 minutes walk)
Nearest Bus Station: Temporary station at Waterloo Place
Club Shop: Famous Five Stand
Opening Times: Monday to Friday 9.00am – 5.00pm,
Matchdays 9.00am to kick-off and ½ hour after the game,
Non-matchday Saturdays 9.30am – 2.00pm
Telephone Nº: (0131) 656-7078
Police Telephone Nº: (0131) 554-9350

GROUND INFORMATION

Away Supporters' Entrances & Sections:
South Stand entrances and accommodation

ADMISSION INFO (2003/2004 PRICES)

Adult Seating: £17.00 – £25.00
Child Seating: £10.00
Programme Price: £2.00

DISABLED INFORMATION

Wheelchairs: 56 spaces in the West Stand, 11 spaces in the
Famous Five Stand and 11 spaces in the South Stand (Away)
Helpers: One helper admitted per disabled person
Prices: Free for the disabled. Normal prices for helpers
Disabled Toilets: 4 available in the Famous Five and South
Stands, 5 available in the West Stand
Contact: (0131) 661-1875   (Bookings are necessary for
home supporters. Away Supporters should book and pay
through their own club)

Travelling Supporters' Information:
Routes: From the West and North: Take the A90 Queensferry Road to the A902 and continue for 2¼ miles. Turn right into Great
Junction Street and follow into Duke Street then Lochend Road. Turn sharp right into Hawkhill Avenue at Lochend Park and follow
the road into Albion Place for the ground; From the South: Take the A1 through Musselburgh (Milton Road/Willow Brae/Lon-
don Road) and turn right into Easter Road after about 2½ miles. Take the 4th right into Albion Road for the ground.

INVERNESS CALEDONIAN THISTLE FC

Founded: 1994 (**Entered League**: 1994)
Former Names: Caledonian Thistle FC
Nickname: 'The Jags' 'Caley'
Ground: Caledonian Stadium, East Longman, Inverness   IV1 1FF
Ground Capacity: 6,500
Seating Capacity: 2,200
Record Attendance: 6,290

Pitch Size: 115 × 75 yards
Colours: Shirts are Royal Blue with a Red side panel, Royal Blue shorts
Telephone Nº: (01463) 222880 (Ground)
Ticket Office: (01463) 222880
Fax Number: (01463) 715816
Web Site: www.sportnetwork.net/main/s14.htm

GENERAL INFORMATION

Car Parking: At the ground
Coach Parking: At the ground
Nearest Railway Station: Inverness (1 mile)
Nearest Bus Station: Inverness
Club Shop: At the ground (Matchdays only)
Weekdays only – Inverness Courier Offices, Stadium Road, Inverness
Opening Times: Weekdays and Matchdays 9.00am–5.00pm
Telephone Nº: (01463) 233059
Police Telephone Nº: (01463) 715555

GROUND INFORMATION

Away Supporters' Entrances & Sections:
Accommodation on the East Side of the Main Stand

ADMISSION INFO (2003/2004 PRICES)

Adult Standing: £9.00
Adult Seating: £11.00
Child Standing: £3.00
Child Seating: £6.00
Programme Price: £1.50

DISABLED INFORMATION

Wheelchairs: 16 spaces available in total
Helpers: Admitted
Prices: Free of charge for the disabled. £11.00 for helpers
Disabled Toilets: Available
Contact: (01463) 222880   (Bookings are necessary)

Travelling Supporters' Information:
Routes: The ground is adjacent to Kessock Bridge. From the South: Take the A9 to Inverness and turn right at the roundabout before the bridge over the Moray Firth; From the North: Take the A9 over the bridge and turn left at the roundabout for the ground.

KILMARNOCK FC

Founded: 1869 (**Entered League**: 1896)
Nickname: 'Killie'
Ground: Rugby Park, Rugby Road, Kilmarnock, Ayrshire   KA1 2DP
Record Attendance: 34,246 (17/8/63)
Pitch Size: 115 × 74 yards

Colours: Blue shirts with broad White stripes, Blue shorts with White trim
Telephone Nº: (01563) 545300
Fax Number: (01563) 522181
Ground Capacity: 18,128 (all seats)
Web Site: www.kilmarnockfc.co.uk

GENERAL INFORMATION

Car Parking: At the ground (Permit Holders only)
Coach Parking: Fairyhill Road Bus Park
Nearest Railway Station: Kilmarnock (15 minutes walk)
Nearest Bus Station: Kilmarnock (10 minutes walk)
Club Shop: In the West Stand at the ground
Opening Times: Monday to Friday 9.00am – 5.00pm, Saturdays 10.00am – 2.00pm
Telephone Nº: (01563) 545310
Police Telephone Nº: (01563) 521188

GROUND INFORMATION

Away Supporters' Entrances & Sections:
Rugby Road turnstiles for the Chadwick Stand

ADMISSION INFO (2003/2004 PRICES)

Adult Seating: £18.00   (£22.00 against the Old Firm)
Concessionary Seating: £12.00
Under 16s Seating: £1.00 in Moffat Stand
Programme Price: £2.00

DISABLED INFORMATION

Wheelchairs: 15 spaces each for home and away fans in the Main Stand
Helpers: One helper admitted per wheelchair
Prices: £5.00 for the disabled. Helpers £8.00
Disabled Toilets: 2 available in the Chadwick Stand and Moffat Stand
Contact: (01563) 527990   (Bookings are necessary)

Travelling Supporters' Information:
Routes: From Glasgow/Ayr: Take the A77 Kilmarnock Bypass. Exit at the Bellfield Interchange. Take the A71 (Irvine) to the first roundabout then take the A759 (Kilmarnock Town Centre). The ground is ½ mile on the left hand side.

LIVINGSTON FC

Founded: 1943 (**Entered League**: 1974)
Former Names: Ferranti Thistle FC, Meadowbank Thistle FC
Nickname: 'The Lions'
Ground: The City Stadium, Alderstone Road, Livingston   EH54 7DN
Ground Capacity: 10,006 (All seats)

Record Attendance: 10,006 (vs Rangers)
Pitch Size: 105 × 72 yards
Colours: Shirts are White with Gold trim, White shorts
Telephone Nº: (01506) 417000
Ticket Office: (01506) 417000
Fax Number: (01506) 418888
Web Site: www.livingstonfc.co.uk

GENERAL INFORMATION
Car Parking: Car Park at the ground by arrangement
Coach Parking: At the ground
Nearest Railway Station: Livingston
Nearest Bus Station: Livingston
Club Shop: At ASDA in Livingston
Opening Times: Daily
Police Telephone Nº: (01506) 431200

GROUND INFORMATION
Away Supporters' Entrances & Sections:
North Stand entrances and accommodation

ADMISSION INFO (2003/2004 PRICES)
Adult Seating: £17.00 – £19.00
Child Seating: £10.00
Note: Prices vary according to the category of the game
Programme Price: £2.00

DISABLED INFORMATION
Wheelchairs: Accommodated
Helpers: Please phone the club for information
Prices: Please phone the club for information
Disabled Toilets: Available
Contact: (01506) 417000   (Bookings are necessary)

Travelling Supporters' Information:
Routes: Exit the M8 at the Livingston turn-off and take the A899 to the Cousland Interchange. Turn right into Cousland Road, pass the Hospital, then turn left into Alderstone Road and the stadium is on the left opposite the Campus.

MONTROSE FC

Founded: 1879 (**Entered League**: 1929)
Nickname: 'Gable Endies'
Ground: Links Park Stadium, Wellington Street, Montrose   DD10 8QD
Ground Capacity: 3,292
Seating Capacity: 1,334
Record Attendance: 8,983 (17/3/73)

Pitch Size: 113 × 70 yards
Colours: Royal Blue shirts with Blue shorts
Telephone Nº: (01674) 673200
Ticket Office: (01674) 673200
Fax Number: (01674) 677311
Web Site: www.montrosefc.co.uk

GENERAL INFORMATION
Car Parking: At the ground and Street parking also
Coach Parking: Mid-Links
Nearest Railway Station: Montrose Western Road
Nearest Bus Station: High Street, Montrose
Club Shop: At the ground
Opening Times: Matchdays only
Telephone Nº: (01674) 673200
Police Telephone Nº: (01674) 672222

GROUND INFORMATION
Away Supporters' Entrances & Sections:
No usual segregation

ADMISSION INFO (2003/2004 PRICES)
Adult Standing: £8.00
Adult Seating: £8.00
Child Standing: £4.00
Child Seating: £4.00
Programme Price: £1.00

DISABLED INFORMATION
Wheelchairs: 5 spaces available in the Main Stand
Helpers: Please phone the club for information
Prices: Please phone the club for information
Disabled Toilets: 2 available in the Main Stand
Contact: (01674) 673200   (Bookings are helpful)

Travelling Supporters' Information:
Routes: Take the main A92 Coastal Road to Montrose. Once in the town, the ground is well signposted and is situated in the Mid-Links area.

MOTHERWELL FC

Founded: 1886 (**Entered League**: 1893)
Nickname: 'The Well'
Ground: Firpark, Firpark Street, Motherwell, ML1 2QN
Ground Capacity: 13,742 (all seats)
Record Attendance: 35,632 (12/3/52)
Pitch Size: 110 × 75 yards

Colours: Shirts are Amber with a Claret hoop, Shorts are white
Telephone Nº: (01698) 333333
Ticket Office: (01698) 338010
Fax Number: (01698) 338001
Web Site: www.motherwellfc.co.uk

GENERAL INFORMATION

Car Parking: Street parking and nearby Car Parks
Coach Parking: Orbiston Street
Nearest Railway Station: Airbles (1 mile)
Nearest Bus Station: Motherwell
Club Shop: At the ground
Opening Times: Tuesdays, Thursdays, Fridays and Saturday Matchdays from 10.00am to 3.00pm
Telephone Nº: (01698) 338025
Police Telephone Nº: (01698) 483000

GROUND INFORMATION

Away Supporters' Entrances & Sections:
Dalziel Drive entrances for the South Stand

ADMISSION INFO (2003/2004 PRICES)

Adult Seating: £13.00 – £19.00
Child Seating: £4.00 – £8.00
Concessionary Seating: £8.00 – £12.00
Note: Discounts are available in the Family Section and prices vary depending on the category of the game
Programme Price: £1.50

DISABLED INFORMATION

Wheelchairs: 20 spaces for home fans and 10 spaces for away fans in the South-West enclosure.
Helpers: Admitted
Prices: Please phone the club for information
Disabled Toilets: One available close to the Disabled Area
Contact: (01698) 333333   (Must book 1 week in advance)

Travelling Supporters' Information:
Routes: From the East: Take the A723 into Merry Street and turn left into Brandon Street (1 mile). Follow through to Windmill Hill Street and turn right at the Fire Station into Knowetop Avenue for the ground; From Elsewhere: Exit the M74 at Junction 4 and take the A723 Hamilton Road into the Town Centre. Turn right into West Hamilton Street and follow into Brandon Street – then as from the East.

PARTICK THISTLE FC

Founded: 1876 (**Entered League**: 1890)
Nickname: 'The Jags'
Ground: Firhill Stadium, 80 Firhill Road, Glasgow, G20 7AL
Ground Capacity: 13,141
Seating Capacity: 10,921
Record Attendance: 49,838 (18/2/22)

Pitch Size: 110 × 75 yards
Colours: Red and Yellow striped shirts, Red shorts
Telephone N°: (0141) 579-1971
Ticket Office: (0141) 579-1971
Fax Number: (0141) 945-1525
Web Site: www.ptfc.co.uk
Club Call N°: (09068) 666474

GENERAL INFORMATION

Car Parking: Street parking
Coach Parking: Panmure Street
Nearest Railway Station: Maryhill
Nearest Underground Station: St. George's Cross
Club Shops: At the Stadium
Opening Times: Matchdays 12.00pm to 5.00pm or 5.30pm to 9.30pm for Night matches. Also Tuesdays 12.30pm to 4.30pm
Telephone N°: (0141) 579-1971
Police Telephone N°: (0141) 532-3700

GROUND INFORMATION

Away Supporters' Entrances & Sections:
North Stand (enter via Firhill Road turnstiles)

ADMISSION INFO (2003/2004 PRICES)

Adult Seating: £16.00
Senior Citizen/Child Seating: £9.00
Programme Price: £2.50

DISABLED INFORMATION

Wheelchairs: 17 spaces in the North Enclosure
Helpers: One helper admitted per wheelchair
Prices: Free for the disabled and one helper
Disabled Toilets: Available in the North Enclosure and the North Stand
Contact: (0141) 579-1971 (Bookings are necessary)

Travelling Supporters' Information:
Routes: From the East: Exit the M8 at Junction 16; From the West: Exit the M8 at Junction 17. From both directions, follow Maryhill Road to Queen's Cross and the ground is on the right.

PETERHEAD FC

Founded: 1891   (**Entered League**: 2000)
Nickname: 'Blue Toon'
Ground: Balmoor Stadium, Peterhead   AB42 1EU
Ground Capacity: 4,000
Seating Capacity: 980
Record Attendance: 2,300
Pitch Size: 110 × 74 yards
Colours: Shirts and Shorts are Royal Blue with White piping

Telephone Nº: (01779) 478256
Fax Number: (01779) 490682
Contact Address: G. Moore, 23 Willowbank Road, Peterhead   AB42 2FG
Contact Phone Nº: (01779) 476870 (Home) or (01224) 820851 (Work)
Web Site: www.peterheadfootballclub.co.uk

GENERAL INFORMATION

Car Parking: At the ground
Coach Parking: At the ground
Nearest Railway Station: Aberdeen
Nearest Bus Station: Peterhead
Club Shop: At the ground
Opening Times: Monday to Saturday 9.00am to 5.00pm
Telephone Nº: (01779) 478256
Police Telephone Nº: (01779) 472571

GROUND INFORMATION

Away Supporters' Entrances & Sections:
Segregation only used when required which is very rare

ADMISSION INFO (2003/2004 PRICES)

Adult Standing: £8.00
Adult Seating: £8.00
Child Standing: £4.00
Child Seating: £4.00
Programme Price: £1.50

DISABLED INFORMATION

Wheelchairs: Accommodated
Helpers: Please phone the club for details
Prices: Please phone the club for details
Disabled Toilets: Available
Contact: (01779) 473434   (Bookings are necessary)

Travelling Supporters' Information:
Routes: The ground is situated on the left of the main road from Fraserburgh (A952), about 300 yards past the swimming pool.

QUEEN OF THE SOUTH FC

Founded: 1919 (**Entered League**: 1923)
Nickname: 'The Doonhamers'
Ground: Palmerston Park, Terregles Street, Dumfries, DG2 9BA
Ground Capacity: 6,412
Seating Capacity: 3,509
Record Attendance: 26,552 (23/2/52)

Pitch Size: 112 × 73 yards
Colours: Blue shirts and shorts
Telephone Nº: (01387) 254853
Ticket Office: (01387) 254853
Fax Number: (01387) 254853
Web Site: www.qosfc.co.uk

GENERAL INFORMATION

Car Parking: Car Park adjacent to the ground
Coach Parking: Car Park adjacent to the ground
Nearest Railway Station: Dumfries (¾ mile)
Nearest Bus Station: Dumfries Whitesands (5 minutes walk)
Club Shop: At the ground
Opening Times: Daily
Telephone Nº: (01387) 254853
Police Telephone Nº: (01387) 252112

GROUND INFORMATION

Away Supporters' Entrances & Sections:
Terregles Street entrances for the East Stand

ADMISSION INFO (2003/2004 PRICES)

Adult Standing: £10.00
Adult Seating: £12.00
Child/Senior Citizen Standing: £6.00
Child Seating: £6.00
Programme Price: £1.20

DISABLED INFORMATION

Wheelchairs: Accommodated in front of the East Stand
Helpers: Please phone the club for details
Prices: Please phone the club for details
Disabled Toilets: One available in the East Stand
Contact: (01387) 254853 (Bookings are necessary)

Travelling Supporters' Information:
Routes: From the East: Take the A75 to Dumfries and follow the ring road over the River Nith. Turn left at the 1st roundabout then right at the 2nd roundabout (the Kilmarnock/Glasgow Road roundabout). The ground is a short way along adjacent to the Tesco store; From the West: Take the A75 to Dumfries and proceed along ring road to the 1st roundabout (Kilmarnock/Glasgow Road) then as from the East; From the North: Take the A76 to Dumfries and carry straight across 1st roundabout for the ground.

QUEEN'S PARK FC

Founded: 1867 (**Entered League**: 1900)
Nickname: 'The Spiders'
Ground: Hampden Park, Mount Florida, Glasgow, G42 9BA
Ground Capacity: 52,000 (All seats)
Record Attendance: 150,239 (17/4/37)

Pitch Size: 115 × 75 yards
Colours: Black and White hooped shirts, White shorts
Telephone Nº: (0141) 632-1275
Ticket Office: (0141) 632-1275
Fax Number: (0141) 636-1612
Web Site: www.queensparkfc.co.uk

GENERAL INFORMATION

Car Parking: Car Park at the Stadium
Coach Parking: Car Park at the Stadium
Nearest Railway Station: Mount Florida and King's Park (both 5 minutes walk)
Nearest Bus Station: Buchanan Street
Club Shop: At the ground
Opening Times: During home matches only
Telephone Nº: (0141) 632-1275
Police Telephone Nº: (0141) 532-4900

GROUND INFORMATION

Away Supporters' Entrances & Sections: South Stand

ADMISSION INFO (2003/2004 PRICES)

Adult Seating: £8.00
Child Seating: £2.00
Parent & Child Seating: £9.00 + £1.00 per additional child
Programme Price: £2.00
Note: Only the South Stand is presently used for games

DISABLED INFORMATION

Wheelchairs: 160 spaces available in total
Helpers: Admitted
Prices: Free for the disabled. Helpers normal prices
Disabled Toilets: Available
Contact: (0141) 632-1275 (Bookings are necessary)

Travelling Supporters' Information:
Routes: From the South: Take the A724 to the Cambuslang Road and at Eastfield branch left into Main Street and follow through Burnhill Street and Westmuir Place into Prospecthill Road. Turn left into Aikenhead Road and right into Mount Annan for Kinghorn Drive and the Stadium; From the South: Take the A77 Fenwick Road, through Kilmarnock Road into Pollokshaws Road then turn right into Langside Avenue. Pass through Battle Place to Battlefield Road and turn left into Cathcart Road. Turn right into Letherby Drive, right into Carmunnock Road and 1st left into Mount Annan Drive for the Stadium; From the North & East: Exit M8 Junction 15 and passing Infirmary on left proceed into High Street and cross the Albert Bridge into Crown Street. Join Cathcart Road and proceed South until it becomes Carmunnock Road. Turn left into Mount Annan Drive and left again into Kinghorn Drive for the Stadium.

RAITH ROVERS FC

Founded: 1883 (**Entered League**: 1902)
Nickname: 'The Rovers'
Ground: Stark's Park, Pratt Street, Kirkcaldy, KY1 1SA
Ground Capacity: 10,104 (All seats)
Record Attendance: 31,306 (7/2/53)
Pitch Size: 113 × 67 yards

Colours: Navy shirts with White bands across chest, White shorts with Navy trim
Telephone N°: (01592) 263514
Ticket Office: (01592) 263514
Fax Number: (01592) 642833
Web Site: www.rrfc.co.uk

GENERAL INFORMATION

Car Parking: Esplanade and Beveridge Car Park
Coach Parking: Railway Station & Esplanade
Nearest Railway Station: Kirkcaldy (15 minutes walk)
Nearest Bus Station: Kirkcaldy (15 minutes walk)
Club Shop: At the ground (matchdays only) and also at Mercat Shopping Centre, Kirkcaldy (before Christmas only)
Opening Times: Monday to Saturday
Telephone N°: (01592) 263514
Police Telephone N°: (01592) 418700

GROUND INFORMATION

Away Supporters' Entrances & Sections:
North Stand and part of the Railway Stand

ADMISSION INFO (2003/2004 PRICES)

Adult Seating: £12.00
Senior Citizen/Child Seating: £5.00
Note: One adult and one child are admitted for £15.00
Programme Price: £1.50

DISABLED INFORMATION

Wheelchairs: 12 spaces each for home and away fans accommodated in the North & South Stands
Helpers: One helper admitted per wheelchair
Prices: Free of charge for the disabled. Helpers pay concessionary prices
Disabled Toilets: Available in the North and South Stands
Are Bookings Necessary: Only for all-ticket games
Contact: (01592) 263514

Travelling Supporters' Information:
Routes: Take the M8 to the end then follow the A90/M90 over the Forth Road Bridge. Exit the M90 at Junction 1 and follow the A921 to Kirkcaldy. On the outskirts of town, turn left at the B & Q roundabout from which the floodlights can be seen. The ground is raised on the hill nearby.

RANGERS FC

Founded: 1873 (**Entered League**: 1890)
Nickname: 'The Gers' 'Light Blues'
Ground: Ibrox Stadium, 150 Edmiston Drive,
Glasgow G51 2XD
Ground Capacity: 50,444 (All seats)
Record Attendance: 118,567 (2/1/39)
Pitch Size: 125 × 89 yards

Colours: Shirts are Blue with White collar and trim,
White shorts
Telephone Nº: (0870) 600-1972
Ticket Office: (0870) 600-1993
Fax Number: (0870) 600-1978
Web Site: www.rangers.co.uk

GENERAL INFORMATION
Car Parking: Albion Car Park
Coach Parking: By Police direction
Nearest Railway Station: Ibrox (Underground) 2 mins. walk
Nearest Bus Station: Glasgow City Centre
Club Shop: The Rangers Superstore, Ibrox Stadium
Opening Times: Monday to Saturday 9.00am to
5.30pm; Sundays 11.00am to 5.00pm and also open one
hour after the end of the game
Telephone Nº: (0141) 427-3710
Police Telephone Nº: (0141) 445-1113

GROUND INFORMATION
Away Supporters' Entrances & Sections:
Broomloan Road Turnstiles for Broomloan Road Stand

ADMISSION INFO (2003/2004 PRICES)
Adult Seating: £19.00 – £22.00
Child Seating: £11.00
Other Concessions: £11.00
Note: Most of the seats are taken by season-ticket holders
Programme Price: £2.00

DISABLED INFORMATION
Wheelchairs: 60 spaces for home fans, 5 for away fans in
front of the West Enclosure
Helpers: Admitted
Prices: Free of charge for the disabled and helpers if they are
members of the Disabled Supporters' Club
Disabled Toilets: Available in the West Enclosure
Contact: (0141) 580-8500 (Bookings are necessary)

Travelling Supporters' Information:
Routes: From All Parts: Exit the M8 at Junction 23. The road leads straight to the Stadium.

ROSS COUNTY FC

Founded: 1929 (**Entered League**: 1994)
Nickname: 'The County'
Ground: Victoria Park, Dingwall, Ross-shire, IV15 9QW
Ground Capacity: 6,500
Seating Capacity: 1,519
Record Attendance: 10,000 (19/2/66)

Pitch Size: 110 × 75 yards
Colours: Navy Blue shirts with White shorts
Telephone Nº: (01349) 860860
Ticket Office: (01349) 860860
Fax Number: (01349) 866277
Web Site: www.rosscountyfootballclub.co.uk

GENERAL INFORMATION

Car Parking: At the ground
Coach Parking: At the ground
Nearest Railway Station: Dingwall (adjacent)
Nearest Bus Station: Dingwall
Club Shop: At the ground
Opening Times: Weekdays and Matchdays
Telephone Nº: (01349) 862233
Police Telephone Nº: (01349) 862444

GROUND INFORMATION

Away Supporters' Entrances & Sections:
East Stand entrances and accommodation

ADMISSION INFO (2003/2004 PRICES)

Adult Standing: £11.00
Adult Seating: £13.00
Child Standing: £6.00
Child Seating: £7.00
Programme Price: £1.00

DISABLED INFORMATION

Wheelchairs: 6 spaces each for home and away fans
Helpers: Admitted
Prices: Normal prices are charged
Disabled Toilets: Available at the bottom of the West Stand
Contact: (01349) 862253 (Bookings are necessary)

Travelling Supporters' Information:
Routes: The ground is situated at Dingwall adjacent to the Railway Station which is down Jubilee Park Road at the bottom of the High Street.

ST. JOHNSTONE FC

Founded: 1884 (**Entered League**: 1911)
Nickname: 'Saints'
Ground: McDiarmid Park, Crieff Road, Perth, PH1 2SJ
Ground Capacity: 10,721 (All seats)
Record Attendance: 10,545 (23/5/99)
Pitch Size: 115 × 75 yards

Colours: Blue shirts and shorts
Telephone Nº: (01738) 459090
Ticket Office: (01738) 455000
Fax Number: (01738) 625771
Web Site: www.stjohnstonefc.co.uk

GENERAL INFORMATION

Car Parking: Car park at the ground
Coach Parking: At the ground
Nearest Railway Station: Perth (3 miles)
Nearest Bus Station: Perth (3 miles)
Club Shop: At the ground
Opening Times: 9.00am to 5.00pm
Telephone Nº: (01738) 459090
Police Telephone Nº: (01738) 621141

GROUND INFORMATION

Away Supporters' Entrances & Sections:
North Stand and North End of the West Stand when appropriate

ADMISSION INFO (2003/2004 PRICES)

Adult Seating: £15.00 – £17.00
Child Seating: £3.00 – £10.00
Other Concessions: £4.00 – £10.00
Programme Price: £2.00

DISABLED INFORMATION

Wheelchairs: 10 spaces each available for home and away fans in the East and West Stands
Helpers: Please phone the club for details
Prices: Please phone the club for details
Disabled Toilets: 2 are available in the East and West Stands
Contact: (01738) 459090 (Bookings are necessary)

Travelling Supporters' Information:
Routes: Follow the M80 to Stirling, take the A9 Inverness Road north from Perth and follow the signs for the 'Football Stadium'. The ground is situated beside a dual-carriageway – the Perth Western By-pass near Junction 11 of the M90.

ST. MIRREN FC

Founded: 1877 (**Entered League**: 1890)
Nickname: 'The Saints' 'The Buddies'
Ground: St.Mirren Park, Love Street, Paisley, PA3 2EJ
Ground Capacity: 10,800 (all seats)
Record Attendance: 47,428 (7/3/25)
Pitch Size: 110 × 70 yards

Colours: Black and White striped shirts, White shorts
Telephone Nº: (0141) 889-2558
Fax Number: (0141) 848-6444
Web Site: www.saintmirren.net

GENERAL INFORMATION

Car Parking: Street parking
Coach Parking: Clark Street (off Greenock Road – 300 yards)
Nearest Railway Station: Paisley Gilmour Street (400 yards)
Nearest Bus Station: Paisley
Club Shop: Provan Sports, Causeyside Street, Paisley
Opening Times: Daily
Telephone Nº: (0141) 889-1629
Police Telephone Nº: (0141) 889-1113

GROUND INFORMATION

Away Supporters' Entrances & Sections:
Entrances on West of Main Stand for West Stand

ADMISSION INFO (2003/2004 PRICES)

Adult Seating: £12.00
Child Seating: £7.00
Note: Special Family Tickets are available
Programme Price: £2.00

DISABLED INFORMATION

Wheelchairs: Accommodated in the West Stand
Helpers: Admitted
Prices: Free of charge for both disabled and helpers
Disabled Toilets: 2 available in the West Stand
Contact: (0141) 840-1337   (Bookings are necessary)

Travelling Supporters' Information:
Routes: From All Parts: Exit the M8 at Junction 29 and take the A726 Greenock Road. The ground is approximately ½ mile along on the left – the floodlights make it clearly visible from some distance.

STENHOUSEMUIR FC

Founded: 1884 (**Entered League**: 1921)
Former Names: Heather Rangers FC
Nickname: 'Warriors'
Ground: Ochilview Park, Gladstone Road, Stenhousemuir   FK5 5QL
Ground Capacity: 2,654
Seating Capacity: 628

Record Attendance: 12,500 (11/3/50)
Pitch Size: 110 × 72 yards
Colours: Maroon shirts with White shorts
Telephone Nº: (01324) 562992
Ticket Office: (01324) 562992
Fax Number: (01324) 562980
Web Site: www.stenhousemuirfc.com

GENERAL INFORMATION

Car Parking: A Large Car Park is adjacent
Coach Parking: Behind the North Terracing
Nearest Railway Station: Larbert (1 mile)
Nearest Bus Station: Falkirk (2½ miles)
Club Shop: At the ground
Opening Times: Weekdays from 9.00am to 5.00pm and also 4 hours before and after home games
Telephone Nº: (01324) 562992
Police Telephone Nº: (01324) 562112

GROUND INFORMATION

Away Supporters' Entrances & Sections:
Terracing entrances and accommodation

ADMISSION INFO (2003/2004 PRICES)

Adult Standing: £8.00
Adult Seating: £9.00
Senior Citizen/Child Standing: £5.00
Senior Citizen/Child Seating: £4.50
Note: Additional Family Discounts are available
Programme Price: £1.30

DISABLED INFORMATION

Wheelchairs: Accommodated
Helpers: Admitted
Prices: Normal prices are charged
Disabled Toilets: Available in the Gladstone Road Stand
Contact: (01324) 562992 (Bookings are not necessary)

Travelling Supporters' Information:
Routes: Exit the M876 at Junction 2 and follow signs for Stenhousemuir. Pass the Old Hospital and turn right after the Golf Course. The ground is on the left behind the houses – the floodlights are visible for ¼ mile.

STIRLING ALBION FC

Founded: 1945 (**Entered League**: 1946)
Nickname: 'The Albion'
Ground: Forthbank Stadium, Spring Kerse, Stirling, FK7 7UJ
Ground Capacity: 3,808
Seating Capacity: 2,508
Record Attendance: 3,808 (17/2/96)

Pitch Size: 110 × 74 yards
Colours: Shirts are Red with White trim, Red Shorts
Telephone Nº: (01786) 450399
Ticket Office: (01786) 450399
Fax Number: (01786) 448400
Web Site: www.stirlingalbionfc.co.uk

GENERAL INFORMATION
Car Parking: Large Car Park adjacent to the ground
Coach Parking: Adjacent to the ground
Nearest Railway Station: Stirling (2 miles)
Nearest Bus Station: Stirling (2 miles)
Club Shop: At the ground
Opening Times: Matchdays Only
Telephone Nº: (01786) 450399
Police Telephone Nº: (01786) 456000

GROUND INFORMATION
Away Supporters' Entrances & Sections:
South Terracing and East Stand

ADMISSION INFO (2003/2004 PRICES)
Adult Standing: £7.00
Adult Seating: £8.00
Child Standing: £4.00
Child Seating: £5.00
Note: Standing admission is only available for certain games.
Family Section: Adult + 1 Child £11.00. Extra children are admitted at £3.00 each up to a maximum of 3 children
Programme Price: £1.00

DISABLED INFORMATION
Wheelchairs: 18 spaces each for home and away fans
Helpers: Admitted
Prices: Free of charge for the disabled and helpers
Disabled Toilets: 2 available beneath each stand
Contact: (01786) 450399 (Bookings are not necessary)

Travelling Supporters' Information:
Routes: Follow signs for Stirling from the M9/M80 Northbound. From Pirnhall Roundabout follow signs for Alloa/St. Andrew's to the 4th roundabout and then turn left for the stadium.

STRANRAER FC

Founded: 1870 (**Entered League**: 1955)
Nickname: 'The Blues'
Ground: Stair Park, London Road, Stranraer, DG9 8BS
Ground Capacity: 5,600
Seating Capacity: 1,900
Record Attendance: 6,500 (24/1/48)

Pitch Size: 110 × 70 yards
Colours: Blue shirts with White shorts
Telephone No: (01776) 703271
Ticket Office: (01776) 703271
Fax Number: (01776) 702194
Web Site: www.stranraerfc.co.uk

GENERAL INFORMATION

Car Parking: Car Park at the ground
Coach Parking: Port Rodie, Stranraer
Nearest Railway Station: Stranraer (1 mile)
Nearest Bus Station: Port Rodie, Stranraer
Club Shop: At the ground
Opening Times: 2.30pm to 3.00pm and during half-time on Matchdays only
Telephone No: None
Police Telephone No: (01776) 702112

GROUND INFORMATION

Away Supporters' Entrances & Sections:
London Road entrances for the Visitors Stand

ADMISSION INFO (2003/2004 PRICES)

Adult Standing: £8.00
Adult Seating: £10.00
Child Standing: £4.00
Child Seating: £6.00
Programme Price: £1.00

DISABLED INFORMATION

Wheelchairs: 6 spaces each for Home and Away fans in front of the North Stand and South Stand
Helpers: Please phone the club for details
Prices: Please phone the club for details
Disabled Toilets: One in the North and South Stands
Contact: (01776) 702194 (Bookings are necessary)

Travelling Supporters' Information:
Routes: From the West: Take the A75 to Stranraer and the ground is on the left-hand side of the road in a public park shortly after entering the town; From the North: Take the A77 and follow it to where it joins with the A75 (then as West). The ground is set back from the road and the floodlights are clearly visible.

ABERDEEN FC

MERKLAND STAND
FAMILY ENCLOSURE

SOUTH STAND

SOUTH STAND
EAST (Away)

(PITTODRIE STREET)
MAIN STAND

RICHARD DONALD STAND
GOLF ROAD

AIRDRIE UNITED FC

SOUTH STAND

EAST STAND

JACK DALZIEL STAND

NORTH STAND

ALBION ROVERS FC

WEST END

MAIN STREET
GRANDSTAND (Away)

CAR PARK
ALBION STREET

Disabled
Area

EAST END

ALLOA ATHLETIC FC

CLACKMANNAN ROAD

HILTON ROAD

MAIN STAND

ARBROATH FC

CAR PARK

QUEEN'S DRIVE DUNDEE ROAD

AYR UNITED FC

RAILWAY END (Away)

FAMILY STAND
(DISABLED)

MAIN STAND
TRYFIELD PLACE

(Away) | HOME TERRACE

SOMERSET ROAD

BERWICK RANGERS FC

SHIELFIELD TERRACE

POPULAR SIDE TERRACING
(Away)

MAIN STAND (All Seats)
(CAR PARK)

BRECHIN CITY FC

COVERED TERRACING

TERRACING

STAND

TRINITY ROAD SEATED
ENCLOSURE

CELTIC FC

WEST STAND

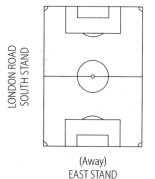

LONDON ROAD
SOUTH STAND

(JANEFIELD STREET)
NORTH STAND

(Away)
EAST STAND

CLYDE FC

SOUTH STAND

OKI MAIN STAND

WEST STAND

COWDENBEATH FC

MAIN STREET
(EAST TERRACING)

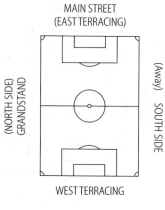

(NORTH SIDE)
GRANDSTAND

(Away)
SOUTH SIDE

WEST TERRACING

DUMBARTON FC

WEST END

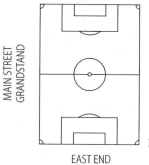

MAIN STREET
GRANDSTAND

CAR PARK
ALBION STREET

EAST END

Disabled
Area

DUNDEE FC

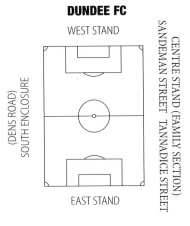

WEST STAND

CENTRE STAND (FAMILY SECTION)
SANDEMAN STREET TANNADICE STREET

(DENS ROAD)
SOUTH ENCLOSURE

EAST STAND

DUNDEE UNITED FC

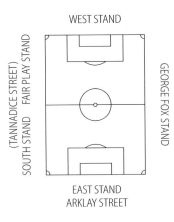

WEST STAND

GEORGE FOX STAND

(TANNADICE STREET)
SOUTH STAND FAIR PLAY STAND

EAST STAND
ARKLAY STREET

DUNFERMLINE ATHLETIC FC

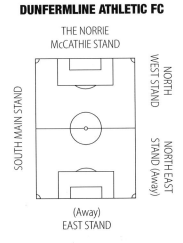

THE NORRIE
McCATHIE STAND

NORTH
WEST STAND

SOUTH MAIN STAND

NORTH EAST
STAND (Away)

(Away)
EAST STAND

EAST FIFE FC

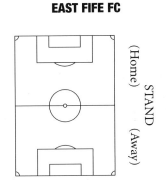

STAND
(Home)
(Away)

EAST STIRLINGSHIRE FC

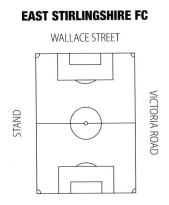

WALLACE STREET

STAND

VICTORIA ROAD

ELGIN CITY FC

SOCIAL CLUB
MAIN STAND

COVERED ENCLOSURE

FALKIRK FC

TRYST ROAD

GLADSTONE ROAD STAND

TERRACING

FORFAR ATHLETIC FC

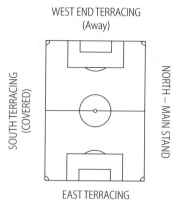

WEST END TERRACING
(Away)

SOUTH TERRACING
(COVERED)

NORTH – MAIN STAND

EAST TERRACING

GREENOCK MORTON FC

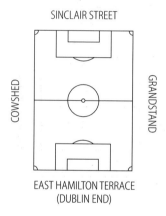

SINCLAIR STREET

COWSHED

GRANDSTAND

EAST HAMILTON TERRACE
(DUBLIN END)

GRETNA FC

LOANWATCH ROAD

DOMINION ROAD

MAIN STAND

CAR PARK

HAMILTON ACADEMICAL FC

RETAIL PARK

MAIN (WEST) STAND

NORTH STAND

HEART OF MIDLOTHIAN FC

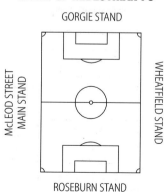

GORGIE STAND

McLEOD STREET
MAIN STAND

WHEATFIELD STAND

ROSEBURN STAND

HIBERNIAN FC

ALBION PLACE
THE FAMOUS FIVE STAND

WEST STAND
(South) (Centre) (North)

EAST SEATED TERRACE

SOUTH STAND LOWER (Away)
SOUTH STAND UPPER (Home)
ALBION ROAD

KILMARNOCK FC

DUNDONALD ROAD END
MOFFAT STAND

EAST STAND

WEST STAND

CHADWICK STAND (Away)
(RUGBY ROAD END)

MONTROSE FC

WELLINGTON STREET

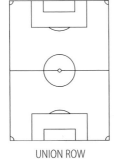

MAIN STAND

WELLINGTON PARK

UNION ROW

INVERNESS CALEDONIAN THISTLE FC

(A9 ROAD)
OPEN TERRACE

MAIN STAND – EAST
(Away)

LIVINGSTON FC

NORTH STAND
(Away)

WEST STAND

EAST STAND (Away)

MOTHERWELL FC

D. COOPER STAND

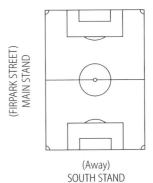

(FIRPARK STREET)
MAIN STAND

EAST STAND

(Away)
SOUTH STAND

PARTICK THISTLE FC

NORTH TERRACING

MAIN STAND
FIRHILL ROAD

JACKIE HUSBAND STAND

SOUTH TERRACING

PETERHEAD FC

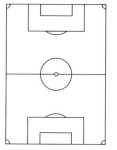

STAND

STAND

QUEEN OF THE SOUTH FC

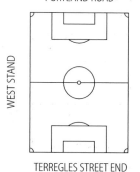

PORTLAND ROAD

WEST STAND

EAST STAND (Away)

TERREGLES STREET END

QUEEN'S PARK FC

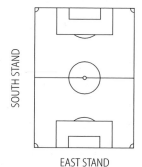

WEST STAND

SOUTH STAND

NORTH STAND

EAST STAND

RAITH ROVERS FC

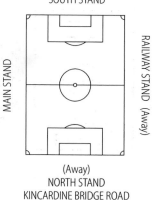

SOUTH STAND

MAIN STAND

RAILWAY STAND (Away)

(Away)
NORTH STAND
KINCARDINE BRIDGE ROAD

RANGERS FC

BROOMLOAN ROAD STAND
(Away)

EDMISTON DRIVE
(EAST) MAIN STAND (WEST)

(WEST) GOVAN STAND (EAST)

COPLAND ROAD STAND

ROSS COUNTY FC

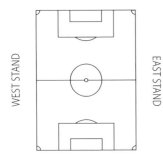

WEST STAND

EAST STAND

ST. JOHNSTONE FC

ORMOND STAND
(FAMILY STAND)

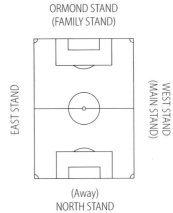

EAST STAND

WEST STAND
(MAIN STAND)

(Away)
NORTH STAND

ST. MIRREN FC

WEST STAND (Away)

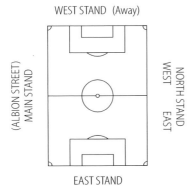

(ALBION STREET)
MAIN STAND

NORTH STAND
WEST
EAST

EAST STAND

STENHOUSEMUIR FC

TRYST ROAD

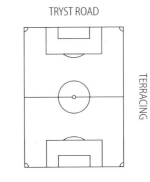

GLADSTONE ROAD STAND

TERRACING

STIRLING ALBION FC

NORTH TERRACING

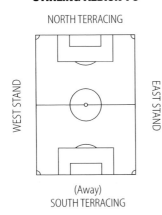

WEST STAND

EAST STAND

(Away)
SOUTH TERRACING

STRANRAER FC

SOUTH STAND

LONDON ROAD (A74)
VISITORS STAND

THE HIGHLAND FOOTBALL LEAGUE

Founded
1893

Secretary
Mr. J.H. Grant

Address
35 Hamilton Drive, Elgin   IV30 2NN

Phone
(01343) 544995

BRORA RANGERS FC

Founded: 1878/79
Nickname: 'The Cattachs'
Ground: Dudgeon Park, Brora   KW9 6QA
Ground Capacity: 4,000
Seating Capacity: 250
Record Attendance: 2,000 (31/8/63)
Pitch Size: 112 × 70 yards

Colours: Shirts are Red with White pinstripes,
Shorts are white
Telephone N°: (01408) 621570
Fax Number: (01408) 621231
Social Club Phone N°: (01408) 621570
Contact Phone N°: (01408) 621231
Web Site: None

GENERAL INFORMATION

Car Parking: Adjacent to the ground
Coach Parking: Adjacent to the ground
Nearest Railway Station: Brora
Nearest Bus Station: Brora
Club Shop: At the ground
Opening Times: Matchdays only
Telephone N°: (01408) 621231
Police Telephone N°: (01408) 621222

GROUND INFORMATION

Away Supporters' Entrances & Sections:
No usual segregation

ADMISSION INFO (2003/2004 PRICES)

Adult Standing: £5.00
Adult Seating: £5.50
Child Standing: £2.00
Child Seating: £2.50
Programme Price: 50p

DISABLED INFORMATION

Wheelchairs: Accommodated
Helpers: Please phone the club for details
Prices: Please phone the club for details
Disabled Toilets: None
Contact: (01408) 621231   (Bookings are necessary)

Travelling Supporters' Information:
Routes: Take the A9 Northbound from Inverness and the Stadium is situated on the right upon entering the town. It is clearly visible from the road.

BUCKIE THISTLE FC

Founded: 1889
Former Names: None
Nickname: 'The Jags'
Ground: Victoria Park, Mid Mar Street, Buckie, Banffshire
Ground Capacity: 5,400
Seating Capacity: 400
Record Attendance: 8,168 (1/3/58)

Pitch Size: 109 × 73 yards
Colours: Green and White hooped shirts, Green shorts
Telephone No: (01542) 836468
Contact Address: Andrew Smith, 49 Archibald Grove, Buckie   AB56 1LG
Contact No: (01542) 839359
Web Site: www.buckiethistle.com

GENERAL INFORMATION

Car Parking: Adjacent to the ground
Coach Parking: Adjacent to the ground
Nearest Railway Station: Keith (12 miles)
Nearest Bus Station: Buckie
Club Shop: None
Social Club: Buckie Thistle Social Club, 3/5 West Church Street, Buckie
Social Club Telephone No: (01542) 832894
Police Telephone No: (01542) 832222

GROUND INFORMATION

Away Supporters' Entrances & Sections:
No usual segregation

ADMISSION INFO (2003/2004 PRICES)

Adult Standing: £5.00
Adult Seating: £6.00
Concessions Standing: £2.00
Concessions Seating: £3.00
Programme Price: £1.00

DISABLED INFORMATION

Wheelchairs: Accommodated when required, but no specific facilities
Helpers: Admitted
Prices: Normal prices apply
Disabled Toilets: None – but available within 100 yards of the ground
Contact: (01542) 886141   (Bookings are helpful)

Travelling Supporters' Information:
Routes: Take the A98 towards Cullen and turn left at Drybridge Crossroads for Buckie Town Centre. After ½ mile, turn left into West Cathcart Street, then left via South Pringle Street to Victoria Park. The ground is situated at the junction of South Pringle Street and Mid Mar Street.

CLACHNACUDDIN FC

Founded: 1886
Nickname: 'Lilywhites'
Ground: Grant Street Park, Wyvis Place, Inverness, IV3 6DR
Ground Capacity: 2,500
Seating Capacity: 154
Record Attendance: 9,000 (27/8/51)
Pitch Size: 108 × 70 yards

Colours: White shirts with Black shorts
Telephone Nº: (01463) 238825
Ticket Information: (01463) 238825
Fax Number: (01463) 718261
Contact Address: M. Mitchell, c/o Club
Contact Phone Nº: (01463) 238825
Web Site: None

GENERAL INFORMATION
Car Parking: Adjacent to the ground
Coach Parking: Adjacent to the ground
Nearest Railway Station: Inverness
Nearest Bus Station: Inverness
Club Shop: At the ground
Opening Times: Matchdays only
Telephone Nº: (01463) 238825
Police Telephone Nº: (01463) 715555

GROUND INFORMATION
Away Supporters' Entrances & Sections:
No usual segregation

ADMISSION INFO (2003/2004 PRICES)
Adult Standing: £5.00
Adult Seating: £6.00
Child Standing: £2.00
Child Seating: £2.00
Programme Price: £1.00

DISABLED INFORMATION
Wheelchairs: Accommodated
Helpers: Admitted
Prices: Normal prices apply
Disabled Toilets: Available
Contact: (01463) 238825 (Bookings are not necessary)

Travelling Supporters' Information:
Routes: From the East and South: From the roundabout at the junction of the A9 and A96, proceed into the Town Centre and over the River Ness. Turn right at the traffic lights (onto the A862 to Dingwall), go up Kenneth Street and over the roundabout onto Telford Street for 200 yards before turning right into Telford Road opposite the Fish Shop. At the top, turn left onto Lower Kessack Street and left again. Finally, turn left into Wyvis Place and the ground is on the left.

COVE RANGERS FC

Founded: 1922
Nickname: None
Ground: Allan Park, Loirston Road, Cove, Aberdeen, AB12 4NS
Ground Capacity: 2,300
Seating Capacity: 200
Record Attendance: 2,300 (15/11/92)
Pitch Size: 104× 65 yards

Colours: Blue shirts and shorts
Telephone Nº: (01224) 871467 (Social Club)
Fax Number: (01224) 895199
Contact Address: Duncan Little, c/o Club
Contact Phone Nº: (01224) 890433 (Matchdays)
Social Club Nº: (01224) 871467
Web Site: www.eteamz.com/coverangers

GENERAL INFORMATION

Car Parking: School Car Park/Loirston Road
Coach Parking: By Police direction
Nearest Railway Station: Guild Street, Aberdeen
Nearest Bus Station: Guild Street, Aberdeen
Club Shop: At the Social Club
Opening Times: Matchdays Only
Telephone Nº: (01224) 871467
Police Telephone Nº: (01224) 639111

GROUND INFORMATION

Away Supporters' Entrances & Sections:
Loirston Road entrances and accommodation

ADMISSION INFO (2003/2004 PRICES)

Adult Standing: £5.00
Adult Seating: £5.00
Child Standing: £2.00
Child Seating: £2.00
Programme Price: 50p

DISABLED INFORMATION

Wheelchairs: Accommodated
Helpers: Admitted
Prices: Free of charge for the disabled
Disabled Toilets: Available in the Social Club
Are Bookings Necessary: No, but preferable
Contact: (01224) 890433 (Duncan Little) (Matchdays); (01224) 896282 (Evenings)

Travelling Supporters' Information:
Routes: From the North: Follow signs to Altens and Cove and take the Cove turn-off at the Skean Dhu Hotel roundabout along Loirston Road – the ground is ½ mile on the right; From the South: Take the Aberdeen Harbour turn-off some 10 miles north of Stonehaven and continue to Skean Dhu Hotel roundabout – then as from the North.
Bus Routes: No.13 bus runs from the City Centre to the ground.

DEVERONVALE FC

Founded: 1938
Nickname: 'The Vale'
Ground: Princess Royal Park, Airlie Gardens, Banff, AB45 1AZ
Ground Capacity: 2,651
Seating Capacity: 418
Record Attendance: 5,000 (27/4/52)
Pitch Size: 109 × 78 yards

Colours: Shirts are Red with White trim, White shorts
Telephone N°: (01261) 818303
Fax Number: (01261) 818303
Contact Address: Stewart McPherson, 8 Victoria Place, Banff AB45 1EL
Contact Phone N°: (01261) 818303
Web Site: www.deveronvale.co.uk

GENERAL INFORMATION

Car Parking: Street parking
Coach Parking: Bridge Road Car Park
Nearest Railway Station: Keith (20 miles)
Nearest Bus Station: Macduff (1 mile)
Club Shop: At the ground
Opening Times: Matchdays only
Telephone N°: (01261) 818303
Police Telephone N°: (01261) 812555

GROUND INFORMATION

Away Supporters' Entrances & Sections:
No usual segregation

ADMISSION INFO (2003/2004 PRICES)

Adult Standing: £5.00
Adult Seating: £6.00
Child Standing: £2.00
Child Seating: £3.00
Programme Price: £1.00

DISABLED INFORMATION

Wheelchairs: Accommodated
Helpers: Admitted
Prices: Please phone the club for details
Disabled Toilets: Available
Contact: (01261) 818303 (Bookings are necessary)

Travelling Supporters' Information:
Routes: From Aberdeen: Take the first exit on the right after Banff Bridge – the ground is situated ½ mile along on the left; From Inverness: Travel through Banff on the main by-pass and take the left turn before Banff Bridge – the ground is ½ mile on the left.

FORRES MECHANICS FC

Founded: 1884
Nickname: 'Can Cans'
Ground: Mosset Park, Lea Road, Forres   IV36 0AU
Ground Capacity: 6,540
Seating Capacity: 540
Record Attendance: 7,000 (2/2/57)
Pitch Size: 106 × 69 yards

Colours: Maroon & Gold striped shirts, Maroon shorts
Telephone/Fax Number: (01309) 675096
Contact Address: David W. Macdonald, Secretary,
7 Brinuth Place, Elgin   IV30 6YW
Contact Phone Nº: (01343) 544294

GENERAL INFORMATION

Car Parking: At the ground
Coach Parking: At the ground
Nearest Railway Station: Forres
Nearest Bus Station: Forres
Club Shop: At the ground
Opening Times: Matchdays only
Telephone Nº: (01309) 675096
Police Telephone Nº: (01309) 672224

GROUND INFORMATION

Away Supporters' Entrances & Sections:
No usual segregation

ADMISSION INFO (2003/2004 PRICES)

Adult Standing: £5.00
Adult Seating: £5.00
Child/O.A.P. Standing: £2.00
Child/O.A.P. Seating: £3.00
Programme Price: £1.00

DISABLED INFORMATION

Wheelchairs: Accommodated
Helpers: Admitted
Prices: Normal prices apply
Disabled Toilets: One available
Contact: (01309) 675096   (Bookings are not necessary)

Travelling Supporters' Information:
Routes: Exit the Forres Bypass (A940) for Grantown on Spey/Forres Town Centre. Take the first left along the burn, cross the bridge then first left for the ground. The ground is clearly visible from the bypass.

FORT WILLIAM FC

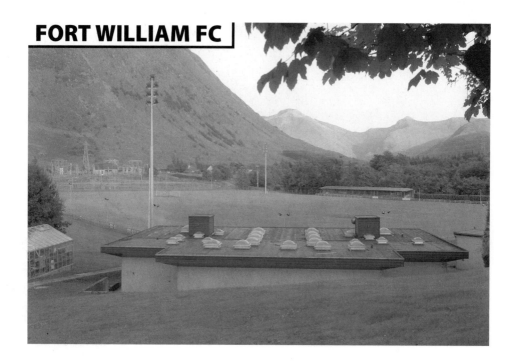

Founded: 1984
Nickname: 'The Fort'
Ground: Claggan Park, Fort William, Inverness-shire
Ground Capacity: 4,600
Seating Capacity: 400
Record Attendance: 1,500 (4/1/86)
Pitch Size: 102 × 80 yards
Colours: Gold and Black shirts with Black shorts

Telephone Nº: None at the ground
Contact Address: J. Campbell, 54 Drumfada Terrace, Corpach, Fort William   PH33 7LA
Contact Phone Nº: (01397) 772298
Contact Fax Number: (01397) 772298
Social Club Number: (01397) 703829
Web Site: www.fortwilliamfc.org.uk

GENERAL INFORMATION

Car Parking: At the ground
Coach Parking: At the ground
Nearest Railway Station: Fort William
Nearest Bus Station: Fort William
Club Shop: None
Police Telephone Nº: (01397) 702361

GROUND INFORMATION

Away Supporters' Entrances & Sections:
No usual segregation

ADMISSION INFO (2003/2004 PRICES)

Adult Standing: £5.00
Adult Seating: £5.00
Child Standing: £2.50 (under 12's are admitted free
Child Seating: £2.50   with a paying adult)
Programme Price: None

DISABLED INFORMATION

Wheelchairs: Accommodated
Helpers: Please phone the club for details
Prices: Please phone the club for details
Disabled Toilets: None
Contact: (01397) 772298   (Bookings are not necessary)

Travelling Supporters' Information:
Routes: From the South: Approaching Fort William on the A82, proceed on the bypass of the Town Centre. After 2 roundabouts continue on Belford Road past the Railway Station on the left and the Swimming Baths on the right. After ½ mile and crossing over the River Nevis, take the first right into Claggan Road and the ground is ½ mile on the left.

FRASERBURGH FC

Founded: 1910
Nickname: 'The Broch'
Ground: Bellslea Park, Seaforth Street, Fraserburgh, AB43 9BD
Ground Capacity: 4,500
Seating Capacity: 480
Record Attendance: 5,800 (13/2/54)
Pitch Size: 106 × 66 yards

Colours: Black and White striped shirts, Black shorts
Telephone Nº: (01346) 518444
Fax Number: –
Contact Address: Finlay Noble, 18 Bawdley Head, Fraserburgh   AB43 9SE
Contact Phone Nº: (01346) 513474
Web Site: www.fraserburghfc.net

GENERAL INFORMATION

Car Parking: At the ground
Coach Parking: At the ground
Nearest Railway Station: Aberdeen (40 miles)
Nearest Bus Station: Fraserburgh
Club Shop: At the ground
Opening Times: Matchdays only
Telephone Nº: (01346) 518444
Police Telephone Nº: (01346) 513121

GROUND INFORMATION

Away Supporters' Entrances & Sections:
No usual segregation

ADMISSION INFO (2003/2004 PRICES)

Adult Standing: £6.00
Adult Seating: £7.00
Child Standing: £3.00
Child Seating: £4.00
Programme Price: £1.00

DISABLED INFORMATION

Wheelchairs: Accommodated
Helpers: Admitted
Prices: Normal prices apply
Disabled Toilets: Available
Contact: (01346) 518444   (Bookings are not necessary)

Travelling Supporters' Information:
Routes: The ground is situated in the Town Centre, off Seaforth Street.

HUNTLY FC

Founded: 1928
Nickname: None
Ground: Christie Park, East Park Street, Huntly, Aberdeenshire AB54 8JE
Ground Capacity: 4,500
Seating Capacity: 270
Record Attendance: 4,500 (18/2/95)
Pitch Size: 105 × 72 yards

Colours: Black and Gold shirts with Black shorts
Telephone Nº: (01466) 793548
Social Club Phone Nº: (01466) 793680
Contact Address: Peter Morrison, Glenlea, Littlejohn Street, Huntly AB54 8HL
Contact Phone Nº: (01466) 793269
Web Site: www.huntlyfc.co.uk

GENERAL INFORMATION

Car Parking: At the ground
Coach Parking: At the ground
Nearest Railway Station: Huntly (1 mile)
Nearest Bus Station: Huntly (¼ mile)
Club Shop: At the ground
Opening Times: Matchdays only
Police Telephone Nº: (01466) 792246

GROUND INFORMATION

Away Supporters' Entrances & Sections:
No usual segregation

ADMISSION INFO (2003/2004 PRICES)

Adult Standing: £5.00
Adult Seating: £6.00
Child Standing: £2.50
Child Seating: £3.50
Programme Price: £1.00

DISABLED INFORMATION

Wheelchairs: Accommodated
Helpers: Please phone the club for details
Prices: Please phone the club for details
Disabled Toilets: None
Contact: (01466) 793269 (Bookings are not necessary)

Travelling Supporters' Information:
Routes: Enter Town off the A96 and proceed along King George V Avenue and Gordon Street. Pass through the Town Centre Square, along Castle Street to East Park Street and the ground is on the right before the Castle.

INVERURIE LOCO WORKS FC

Founded: 1903
Nickname: 'Locos'
Ground: Harlaw Park, Harlaw Road, Inverurie, Aberdeenshire
Ground Capacity: 2,500
Seating Capacity: 250
Record Attendance: 2,150
Pitch Size: 110 × 70 yards

Colours: Red and Black striped shirts, Black shorts
Telephone Nº: (01467) 623055
Fax Number: (01467) 622168
Contact Address: Gordon Park, 13 Golf Crescent, Inverurie AB51 3QU
Contact Phone Nº: (01467) 621347
Web Site: www.eteamz.com/inverurielocoworks

GENERAL INFORMATION
Car Parking: At the ground
Coach Parking: At the ground
Nearest Railway Station: Inverurie
Nearest Bus Station: –
Club Shop: Limited supply of merchandise available

GROUND INFORMATION
Away Supporters' Entrances & Sections:
No usual segregation

ADMISSION INFO (2003/2004 PRICES)
Adult Standing: £5.00
Adult Seating: £5.00
Child/Senior Citizen Standing: £2.00
Child/Senior Citizen Seating: £2.00
Programme Price: £1.00

DISABLED INFORMATION
Wheelchairs: Accommodated in the Covered Enclosure
Helpers: Admitted
Prices: Normal prices apply
Disabled Toilets: Available
Contact: (01467) 621347

Travelling Supporters' Information:
Routes: From the North: Take the A96 to the Inverurie bypass then turn left at the Safeways roundabout along Blackhall Road and left at the next roundabout into Boroughmuir Drive. Cross the next roundabout and then turn 1st right into Hawlaw Road for the ground; From the South: Take the A96 to the Inverurie bypass then as above.

KEITH FC

Founded: 1919
Nickname: 'Maroons'
Ground: Kynoch Park, Balloch Road, Keith AB55 5EN
Ground Capacity: 4,500
Seating Capacity: 450
Record Attendance: 5,820 (4/2/28)
Pitch Size: 110 × 75 yards

Colours: Shirts & shorts are Maroon with Sky Blue trim
Telephone Nº: (01542) 882629
Fax Number: (01542) 882631
Contact Address: A.T.A. Rutherford, c/o Club
Contact Phone Nº: (01542) 882629
Web Site: –

GENERAL INFORMATION

Car Parking: Street parking in Balloch Road, Moss Street and Reidhaven Square
Coach Parking: Balloch Road or Bridge Street Coach Park
Nearest Railway Station: Keith (1 mile)
Nearest Bus Station: Keith
Club Shop: None
Police Telephone Nº: (01542) 882502

GROUND INFORMATION

Away Supporters' Entrances & Sections:
No usual segregation except for some Cup Ties

ADMISSION INFO (2003/2004 PRICES)

Adult Standing: £5.00
Adult Seating: £6.00
Child Standing: £2.00
Child Seating: £3.00
Programme Price: £1.00

DISABLED INFORMATION

Wheelchairs: Accommodated
Helpers: Admitted
Prices: Normal prices apply
Disabled Toilets: None

Travelling Supporters' Information:
Routes: From Aberdeen: Coming in on the A96, turn right up Bridge Street (across from the Bus Stop at Reidhaven Square), then take the first left for Balloch Road; From Inverness: Coming in on the A96, take the second left after the Citroen Keith Garage in Moss Street onto Balloch Road.

LOSSIEMOUTH FC

Founded: 1945
Nickname: 'Coasters'
Ground: Grant Park, Kellas Avenue, Lossiemouth IV31 6JG
Ground Capacity: 3,500
Seating Capacity: 250
Record Attendance: 2,700 (28/12/48)
Pitch Size: 110 × 60 yards

Colours: Red shirts and shorts
Telephone Nº: (01343) 813717
Fax Number: (01343) 815440
Social Club Nº: (01343) 813168
Contact Address: Alan McIntosh, 3 Forties Place, Lossiemouth IV31 6SS
Contact Phone Nº: (01343) 813328 & (07890) 749053
Contact e-mail: alanlfcsec@aol.com

GENERAL INFORMATION
Car Parking: At the ground
Coach Parking: At the ground
Nearest Railway Station: Elgin
Nearest Bus Station: Lossiemouth
Club Shop: At the ground
Opening Times: Matchdays only
Telephone Nº: (01343) 813168
Police Telephone Nº: (01343) 812022

GROUND INFORMATION
Away Supporters' Entrances & Sections:
No usual segregation

ADMISSION INFO (2003/2004 PRICES)
Adult Standing: £5.00
Adult Seating: £5.00
Child Standing: £2.00 (Free when accompanied by adult)
Child Seating: £2.00
Programme Price: 50p

DISABLED INFORMATION
Wheelchairs: Accommodated
Helpers: Admitted
Prices: Free of charge for the disabled
Disabled Toilets: Available
Contact: (01343) 813328 (Alan McIntosh) (Please book)

Travelling Supporters' Information:
Routes: Take the Main Road into Lossiemouth and take the second turning on the right. Turn right again after 100 yards.

NAIRN COUNTY FC

Founded: 1914
Nickname: 'The Wee County'
Ground: Station Park, Balblair Road, Nairn IV12 5LT
Ground Capacity: 3,800
Seating Capacity: 250
Record Attendance: 4,000 (2/9/50)
Pitch Size: 110 × 62 yards

Colours: Yellow shirts with Navy border, Navy shorts
Telephone Nº: (01667) 454298
Fax Number: (01667) 462510
Contact Address: John McNeill, 50 Station Road, Ardersier, Inverness IV2 7ST
Contact Phone Nº: (01667) 462510
Web Site: None

GENERAL INFORMATION

Car Parking: At the ground
Coach Parking: At the ground
Nearest Railway Station: Nairn (adjacent)
Nearest Bus Station: King Street, Nairn (½ mile)
Club Shop: At the Social Club
Opening Times: Club hours only
Telephone Nº: (01667) 453286
Police Telephone Nº: (01667) 452222

GROUND INFORMATION

Away Supporters' Entrances & Sections:
No usual segregation

ADMISSION INFO (2003/2004 PRICES)

Adult Standing: £5.00
Adult Seating: £6.00
Senior Citizen/Child Standing: £2.00
Senior Citizen/Child Seating: £2.50
Programme Price: £1.00

DISABLED INFORMATION

Wheelchairs: Accommodated in the Stand
Helpers: Admitted
Prices: £4.00 for the disabled
Disabled Toilets: None
Contact: (01667) 462510 (Bookings are not necessary)

Travelling Supporters' Information:
Routes: The ground is situated on the south side of Nairn at the bottom of the Main Street, adjacent to the Railway Station.

ROTHES FC

Founded: 1938
Former Names: Rothes Victoria FC
Nickname: 'The Speysiders'
Ground: Mackessack Park, Rothes   AB38 7BY
Ground Capacity: 2,650
Seating Capacity: 160
Record Attendance: 2,054 (September 1946)
Pitch Size: 108 × 74 yards

Colours: Tangerine shirts with Black shorts
Telephone N°: (01340) 831972
Social Club N°: (01340) 831348
Fax Number: None
Contact Address: Neil R. McKenzie, c/o Rothes FC
Social Club, Seafield Square, Rothes
Contact Phone N°: (01340) 831344
Web Site: None

GENERAL INFORMATION

Car Parking: At the ground
Coach Parking: At the ground
Nearest Railway Station: Elgin
Nearest Bus Station: Elgin
Club Shop: None
Nearest Police Station: Rothes
Police Telephone N°: (01340) 831341

GROUND INFORMATION

Away Supporters' Entrances & Sections:
No usual segregation

ADMISSION INFO (2003/2004 PRICES)

Adult Standing: £5.00
Adult Seating: £6.00
Child Standing: £2.00
Child Seating: £2.50
Programme Price: None – Monthly Magazine 50p

DISABLED INFORMATION

Wheelchairs: Accommodated
Helpers: Admitted
Prices: Normal prices apply
Disabled Toilets: Available
Contact: (01340) 831344   (Bookings are not necessary)

Travelling Supporters' Information:
Routes: The ground is next to Grant's Whisky Distillery at the North side of Rothes, by the junction of the Keith and Elgin Roads.

WICK ACADEMY FC

Founded: 1893
Nickname: 'The Scorries'
Ground: Harmsworth Park, South Road, Wick, Caithness KW1 5NH
Ground Capacity: 2,000
Seating Capacity: 433
Record Attendance: 2,000 (30/7/84)
Pitch Size: 106 × 76 yards

Colours: Black and White striped shirts, Black shorts
Telephone Nº: (01955) 602446
Fax Number: (01955) 602446
Contact Address: Mr. A. Carter, 8 Argyle Square, Wick, Caithness KW1 5AL
Contact Phone Nº: (01955) 604275
Web Site: None

GENERAL INFORMATION

Car Parking: At the ground
Coach Parking: At the ground
Nearest Railway Station: Wick (10 minutes walk)
Nearest Bus Station: Wick
Club Shop: Wick Sports Shop, High Street, Wick
Opening Times: 9.00am to 5.00pm
Telephone Nº: (01955) 602930
Police Telephone Nº: (01955) 603551

GROUND INFORMATION

Away Supporters' Entrances & Sections:
No usual segregation

ADMISSION INFO (2003/2004 PRICES)

Adult Standing: £5.00
Adult Seating: £5.00 – £6.00
Child Standing: £2.00
Child Seating: £2.00 – £3.00
Programme Price: 50p

DISABLED INFORMATION

Wheelchairs: 2 spaces available in the North Stand
Helpers: Please phone the club for details
Prices: Please phone the club for details
Disabled Toilets: None
Contact: (01955) 604275 (Bookings are not necessary)

Travelling Supporters' Information:
Routes: The ground is situated on the A99 road from Inverness beside the Cemetery.

BRORA RANGERS FC

SCHOOL END

MAIN STAND

SEAFORTH ENCLOSURE

SOCIAL CLUB
CAR PARK

BUCKIE THISTLE FC

MAIN STAND

COVERED ENCLOSURE

SCHOOL END

CLACHNACUDDIN FC

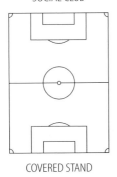

SOCIAL CLUB

COVERED STAND

COVE RANGERS FC

COVERED ENCLOSURE

MAIN STAND

OPEN TERRACING

DEVERONVALE FC

BRIDGE STREET END

MAIN STAND

CANAL PARK BANK

NEW ROAD END

FORRES MECHANICS FC

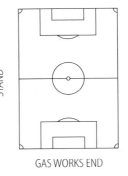

BOGTON END

STAND

CAR PARK

GAS WORKS END

FORT WILLIAM FC

STAND

FRASERBURGH FC

STAND

HUNTLY FC

EAST PARK STREET

COVERED ENCLOSURE

STAND

INVERURIE LOCO WORKS FC

MAIN STAND

KEITH FC

MAIN STAND

COVERED ENCLOSURE

LOSSIEMOUTH FC

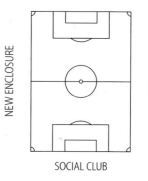

NEW ENCLOSURE

STAND

SOCIAL CLUB

NAIRN COUNTY FC

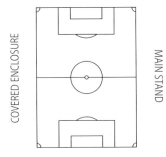

ROTHES FC

WICK ACADEMY FC

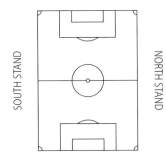

STATISTICS
SEASON 2002/2003

Scottish Premier League
Home & Away Chart • Final League Table

Scottish Football League Division One
Home & Away Chart • Final League Table

Scottish Football League Division Two
Home & Away Chart • Final League Table

Scottish Football League Division Three
Home & Away Chart • Final League Table

Press & Journal Highland Football League
Home & Away Chart • Final League Table

Scottish Cup

Scottish League Cup

Scottish League Challenge Cup

Round 4	22nd Feb 2003	Alloa Athletic	0	Falkirk	2	
Round 4	22nd Feb 2003	Ayr United	0	Rangers	1	
Round 4	23rd Feb 2003	Celtic	3	St. Johnstone	0	
Round 4	22nd Feb 2003	Clyde	0	Motherwell	2	
Round 4	22nd Feb 2003	Dundee	2	Aberdeen	0	
Round 4	22nd Feb 2003	Dunfermline	1	Hibernian	1	
Round 4	22nd Feb 2003	Inverness Caledonian Thistle	6	Hamilton Academical	1	
Round 4	22nd Feb 2003	Morton	0	Stranraer	2	
Replay	6th Mar 2003	Hibernian	0	Dunfermline	2	
Round 5	23rd Mar 2003	Dunfermline	1	Rangers	1	
Round 5	22nd Mar 2003	Falkirk	1	Dundee	1	
Round 5	23rd Mar 2003	Inverness Caledonian Thistle	1	Celtic	0	
Round 5	22nd Mar 2003	Stranraer	0	Motherwell	4	
Replay	9th Apr 2003	Dundee	4	Falkirk	1	(aet)
Replay	9th Apr 2003	Rangers	3	Dunfermline	0	
Semi-Final	20th Apr 2003	Dundee	1	Inverness Caledonian Thistle	0	
Semi-Final	19th Apr 2003	Rangers	4	Motherwell	3	
FINAL	31st May 2003	Rangers	1	Dundee	0	

Scottish League Cup 2002/2003

Round 1	7th Sep 2002	Airdrie United	1	Elgin City	0	
Round 1	7th Sep 2002	Albion Rovers	0	Hamilton Academical	1	
Round 1	7th Sep 2002	Berwick Rangers	4	Arbroath	2	
Round 1	10th Sep 2002	Clyde	0	Ross County	1	
Round 1	10th Sep 2002	Cowdenbeath	3	Montrose	2	
Round 1	10th Sep 2002	Falkirk	2	Peterhead	0	
Round 1	7th Sep 2002	Gretna	1	East Fife	2	
Round 1	10th Sep 2002	Inverness Caledonian Thistle	2	Dumbarton	0	
Round 1	7th Sep 2002	Morton	2	St. Mirren	3	(aet)
Round 1	7th Sep 2002	Queen of the South	2	Forfar Athletic	0	
Round 1	7th Sep 2002	Queen's Park	1	East Stirlingshire	0	
Round 1	10th Sep 2002	Raith Rovers	2	Alloa Athletic	3	(aet)
Round 1	11th Sep 2002	Stirling Albion	3	Stenhousemuir	3	(aet)
		Stirling Albion won on penalties				
Round 1	7th Sep 2002	Stranraer	6	Brechin City	1	
Round 2	24th Sep 2002	Alloa Athletic	0	Hibernian	2	
Round 2	24th Sep 2002	Ayr United	0	Falkirk	2	
Round 2	24th Sep 2002	Berwick Rangers	0	Partick Thistle	3	
Round 2	24th Sep 2002	Cowdenbeath	1	Dunfermline	2	(aet)
Round 2	25th Sep 2002	Dundee	3	Queen of the South	1	
Round 2	24th Sep 2002	Dundee United	4	Queen's Park	1	
Round 2	24th Sep 2002	East Fife	0	Motherwell	2	
Round 2	24th Sep 2002	Inverness Caledonian Thistle	3	St. Mirren	1	
Round 2	24th Sep 2002	Kilmarnock	0	Airdrie United	0	(aet)
		Airdrie United won on penalties				
Round 2	24th Sep 2002	Ross County	3	Hamilton Academical	0	
Round 2	25th Sep 2002	Stirling Albion	2	Heart of Midlothian	3	
Round 2	24th Sep 2002	Stranraer	1	St. Johnstone	3	(aet)
Round 3	6th Nov 2002	Aberdeen	3	Motherwell	1	
Round 3	29th Oct 2002	Airdrie United	1	Dundee United	2	
Round 3	23rd Oct 2002	Celtic	4	Inverness Caledonian Thistle	2	
Round 3	22nd Oct 2002	Dunfermline	2	Falkirk	0	
Round 3	23rd Oct 2002	Heart of Midlothian	3	Ross County	0	
Round 3	24th Oct 2002	Hibernian	2	Rangers	3	
Round 3	22nd Oct 2002	Partick Thistle	1	Dundee	0	
Round 3	5th Nov 2002	St. Johnstone	0	Livingston	1	
Quarter-Final	23th Nov 2002	Aberdeen	0	Heart of Midlothian	1	
Quarter-Final	6th Nov 2002	Celtic	1	Partick Thistle	1	(aet)
		Celtic won on penalties				
Quarter-Final	7th Nov 2002	Dunfermline	0	Rangers	1	
Quarter-Final	13th Nov 2002	Livingston	0	Dundee United	2	
Semi-Final	5th Feb 2003	Celtic	3	Dundee United	0	
Semi-Final	4th Feb 2003	Rangers	1	Heart of Midlothian	0	
FINAL	16th Mar 2003	Rangers	2	Celtic	1	

SCOTLAND INTERNATIONAL LINE-UPS AND STATISTICS 1997-1998

1st June 1997
v MALTA *Valletta*

J. Leighton	Hibernian
C. Burley	Chelsea
T. Boyd	Celtic
B. McAllister	Wimbledon (sub. D. Weir)
C. Dailly	Derby County
T. McKinlay	Celtic
D. Hopkin	Crystal Palace (sub. G. Durie)
K. Gallacher	Blackburn Rov. (sub. S. Gemmill)
D. Jackson	Hibernian
G. McAllister	Coventry City
J. Collins	Monaco (sub. S. Donnelly)

Result 3-2   Jackson 2, Dailly

8th June 1997
v BELARUS *Minsk*

J. Leighton	Hibernian
C. Burley	Chelsea
T. Boyd	Celtic
C. Dailly	Derby County
P. Lambert	Borussia Dortmund
T. McKinlay	Celtic (sub. B. McAllister)
K. Gallacher	Blackburn Rovers
D. Hopkin	Crystal Palace (sub. S. Gemmill)
D. Jackson	Hibernian (sub. W. Dodds)
G. McAllister	Coventry City
G. Durie	Rangers

Result 1-0   G. McAllister (pen)

7th September 1997
v BELARUS *Pittodrie*

J. Leighton	Aberdeen
C. Burley	Celtic
T. McKinlay	Celtic
C. Calderwood	Tottenham Hotspur
T. Boyd	Celtic
C. Dailly	Derby County
P. Lambert	Borussia Dortmund
K. Gallacher	Blackburn Rovers (sub. W. Dodds)
G. Durie	Rangers (sub. A. McCoist)
G. McAllister	Coventry City (sub. D. Hopkin)
J. Collins	Monaco

Result 4-1   Gallacher 2, Hopkin 2

11th October 1997
v LATVIA *Celtic Park*

J. Leighton	Aberdeen
C. Burley	Celtic (sub. W. McKinlay)
T. Boyd	Celtic (sub. T. McKinlay)
C. Calderwood	Tottenham Hotspur
E. Hendry	Blackburn Rovers
C. Dailly	Derby County
P. Lambert	Borussia Dortmund
K. Gallacher	Blackburn Rovers
G. Durie	Rangers (sub. S. Donnelly)
G. McAllister	Coventry City
J. Collins	Monaco

Result 2-0   Gallacher, Durie

12th November 1997
v FRANCE *St. Etienne*

N. Sullivan	Wimbledon
C. Burley	Celtic
T. Boyd	Celtic (sub. T. McKinlay)
C. Calderwood	Tottenham Hotspur
D. Weir	Hearts (sub. M. Elliott)
C. Dailly	Derby County
W. McKinlay	Blackburn Rovers
K. Gallacher	Blackburn Rov. (sub. S. Donnelly)
G. Durie	Rangers (sub. D. Hopkin)
G. McAllister	Coventry City
J. Collins	Monaco

Result 1-2   Durie

22nd April 1998
v FINLAND *Easter Road*

J. Leighton	Aberdeen
C. Calderwood	Tottenham Hotspur (sub. G. Durie)
C. Dailly	Derby County (sub. T. Boyd)
M. Elliott	Leicester City (sub. D. Weir)
E. Hendry	Blackburn Rovers
D. Whyte	Aberdeen
W. McKinlay	Blackburn Rovers
S. Gemmill	Nottm. Forest (sub. P. Lambert)
D. Jackson	Celtic (sub. K. Gallacher)
S. Booth	Bor. Dortmund (sub. S. Donnelly)
J. Collins	Monaco

Result 1-1 Jackson

SCOTLAND INTERNATIONAL LINE-UPS AND STATISTICS 1998

23rd May 1998
v COLOMBIA *New York*
N. Sullivan	Wimbledon
J. McNamara	Celtic (sub. W. McKinlay)
C. Dailly	Derby County
C. Calderwood	Tottenham Hotspur
E. Hendry	Blackburn Rovers
T. Boyd	Celtic
C. Burley	Celtic
P. Lambert	Celtic
G. Durie	Rangers (sub. S. Donnelly)
D. Jackson	Celtic (sub. S. Booth)
J. Collins	Monaco

Result 2-2 Collins, Burley

30th May 1998
v U.S.A. *Washington*
J. Leighton	Aberdeen
T. McKinlay	Celtic (sub. J. McNamara)
C. Dailly	Derby County
C. Calderwood	Tottenham Hotspur
E. Hendry	Blackburn Rovers
T. Boyd	Celtic
W. McKinlay	Blackburn Rovers (sub. C. Burley)
P. Lambert	Celtic
D. Jackson	Celtic
K. Gallacher	Blackburn Rvrs. (sub. S. Donnelly)
J. Collins	Monaco

Result 0-0

10th June 1998
v BRAZIL *St. Denis*
J. Leighton	Aberdeen
C. Burley	Celtic
C. Dailly	Derby County (sub. T. McKinlay)
C. Calderwood	Tottenham Hotspur
E. Hendry	Blackburn Rovers
T. Boyd	Celtic
P. Lambert	Celtic
K. Gallacher	Blackburn Rovers
G. Durie	Rangers
D. Jackson	Celtic (sub. W. McKinlay)
J. Collins	Monaco

Result 1-2 Collins (pen)

590: 16th June 1998
v NORWAY *Bordeaux*
J. Leighton	Aberdeen
C. Burley	Celtic
C. Dailly	Derby County
C. Calderwood	Tottenham Hotspur (sub. D. Weir)
E. Hendry	Blackburn Rovers
T. Boyd	Celtic
P. Lambert	Celtic
K. Gallacher	Blackburn Rovers
G. Durie	Rangers
D. Jackson	Celtic (sub. J. McNamara)
J. Collins	Monaco

Result 1-1 Burley

23rd June 1998
v MOROCCO *St. Etienne*
J. Leighton	Aberdeen
J. McNamara	Celtic (sub. T. McKinlay)
C. Dailly	Derby County
D. Weir	Heart of Midlothian
E. Hendry	Blackburn Rovers
T. Boyd	Celtic
C. Burley	Celtic
P. Lambert	Celtic
G. Durie	Rangers (sub. S. Booth)
K. Gallacher	Blackburn Rovers
J. Collins	Monaco

Result 0-3

5th September 1998
v LITHUANIA (ECQ) *Vilnius*
J. Leighton	Aberdeen
M. Elliott	Leicester City
T. Boyd	Celtic
C. Calderwood	Tottm. Hotspur (sub. C. Davidson)
E. Hendry	Rangers
C. Dailly	Blackburn Rovers
K. Gallacher	Blackburn Rovers
P. Lambert	Celtic
A. McCoist	Kilmarnock (sub. N. McCann)
D. Jackson	Celtic (sub. B. Ferguson)
J. Collins	Everton

Result 0-0

SCOTLAND INTERNATIONAL LINE-UPS AND STATISTICS 1998-1999

10th October 1998
v ESTONIA (ECQ) *Edinburgh*

J. Leighton	Aberdeen
D. Weir	Heart of Midlothian
T. Boyd	Celtic
C. Calderwood	Tott'm Hotspur (sub. S. Donnelly)
E. Hendry	Rangers
C. Davidson	Blackburn Rovers
K. Gallacher	Blackburn Rvrs. (sub. D. Jackson)
W. McKinlay	Blackburn Rovers
A. McCoist	Kilmarnock (sub. W. Dodds)
I. Durrant	Kilmarnock
A. Johnston	Sunderland

Result 3-2 Dodds 2, Hohlov-Simson (own goal)

14th October 1998
v FAROE ISLANDS (ECQ) *Aberdeen*

N. Sullivan	Wimbledon
D. Weir	Heart of Midlothian
T. Boyd	Celtic
M. Elliott	Leicester City
E. Hendry	Rangers
C. Davidson	Blackburn Rovers
W. McKinlay	Blackburn Rovers (sub. I. Durrant)
C. Burley	Celtic
S. Donnelly	Celtic
W. Dodds	Dundee United
A. Johnston	Sunderland (sub. S. Glass)

Result 2-1 Burley, Dodds

31st March 1999
v CZECH REPUBLIC (ECQ) *Celtic Park*

N. Sullivan	Wimbledon
D. Weir	Everton
T. Boyd	Celtic
P. Lambert	Celtic
M. Elliott	Leicester City
C. Davidson	Blackburn Rvrs (sub. A. Johnston)
D. Hopkin	Leeds United
C. Burley	Celtic
E. Jess	Aberdeen
G. McAllister	Coventry City (sub. D. Hutchison)
N. McCann	Rangers

Result 1-2 Jess

28th April 1999
v GERMANY *Bremen*

N. Sullivan	Wimbledon
D. Weir	Everton
E. Hendry	Rangers (sub. P. Ritchie)
T. Boyd	Celtic
S. Gemmill	Everton (sub. E. Jess)
I. Durrant	Kilmarnock (sub. R. Winters)
P. Lambert	Celtic (sub. C. Cameron)
A. Johnston	Sunderland (sub. B. O'Neil)
C. Davidson	Blackburn Rovers (sub. D. Whyte)
D. Hutchison	Everton
W. Dodds	Dundee United

Result 1-0 Hutchison

5th June 1999
v FAROE ISLANDS (ECQ) *Toftir*

N. Sullivan	Wimbledon
D. Weir	Everton
T. Boyd	Celtic
C. Calderwood	Aston Villa
M. Elliott	Leicester City
C. Davidson	Blackburn Rovers
W. Dodds	Dundee United
P. Lambert	Celtic
K. Gallacher	Blackburn Rovers (sub. E. Jess)
I. Durrant	Kilmarnock (sub. C. Cameron)
A. Johnston	Sunderland (sub. S. Gemmill)

Result 1-1 Johnston

9th June 1999
v CZECH REPUBLIC (ECQ) *Prague*

N. Sullivan	Wimbledon
D. Weir	Everton
T. Boyd	Celtic
C. Calderwood	Aston Villa
P. Ritchie	Heart of Midlothian
C. Davidson	Blackburn Rovers
W. Dodds	Dundee United
P. Lambert	Celtic
K. Gallacher	Blackburn Rovers
I. Durrant	Kilmarnock (sub. E. Jess)
A. Johnston	Sunderland

Result 2-3 Ritchie, Johnston

SCOTLAND INTERNATIONAL LINE-UPS AND STATISTICS 1999

4th September 1999
v BOSNIA (ECQ) *Sarajevo*

N. Sullivan	Wimbledon
D. Weir	Everton
D. Hopkin	Leeds United
C. Calderwood	Aston Villa (sub. C. Dailly)
E. Hendry	Rangers
B. Ferguson	Rangers (sub. I. Durrant)
W. Dodds	Rangers
C. Burley	Celtic
N. McCann	Rangers (sub. K. Gallacher)
D. Hutchison	Everton
J. Collins	Everton

Result 2-1 Dodds, Hutchison

8th September 1999
v ESTONIA (ECQ) *Tallinn*

N. Sullivan	Wimbledon
D. Weir	Everton
C. Davidson	Blackburn Rovers
C. Dailly	Blackburn Rovers
E. Hendry	Rangers
I. Durrant	Kilmarnock (sub. B. Ferguson)
W. Dodds	Dundee United
C. Burley	Celtic
A. Johnston	Sunderland (sub. N. McCann)
D. Hutchison	Everton
J. Collins	Everton

Result 0-0

5th October 1999
v BOSNIA (ECQ) *Ibrox*

N. Sullivan	Wimbledon
D. Weir	Everton
C. Davidson	Blackburn Rovers
C. Dailly	Blackburn Rovers
E. Hendry	Rangers (sub. C. Calderwood)
P. Lambert	Celtic
W. Dodds	Dundee Utd. (sub. G. McSwegan)
C. Burley	Celtic
K. Gallacher	Newcastle Utd. (sub. M. Burchill)
D. Hopkin	Leeds United
J. Collins	Everton

Result 1-0 Collins

9th October 1999
v LITHUANIA (ECQ) *Hampden Pk*

J. Gould	Celtic
D. Weir	Everton
C. Davidson	Blackburn Rovers
P. Lambert	Celtic
B. O'Neil	Wolfsburg
P. Ritchie	Heart of Midlothian
C. Dailly	Blackburn Rovers
C. Burley	Celtic (sub. C. Cameron)
M. Burchill	Celtic (sub. W. Dodds)
D. Hutchison	Everton
G. McSwegan	Hearts (sub. K. Gallacher)

Result 3-0 Cameron, Hutchison, McSwegan

13th November 1999
v ENGLAND (EC Play-Off)
Hampden Park

N. Sullivan	Wimbledon
D. Weir	Everton
C. Dailly	Blackburn Rovers
P. Ritchie	Heart of Midlothian
E. Hendry	Rangers
B. Ferguson	Rangers
W. Dodds	Dundee United
C. Burley	Celtic
K. Gallacher	Newcastle Utd. (sub. M. Burchill)
D. Hutchison	Everton
J. Collins	Everton

Result 0-2

604: 17th November 1999
v ENGLAND (EC Play-Off)
Wembley

N. Sullivan	Wimbledon
D. Weir	Everton
C. Davidson	Blackburn Rovers
C. Dailly	Blackburn Rovers
E. Hendry	Rangers
B. Ferguson	Rangers
W. Dodds	Dundee United
C. Burley	Celtic
N. McCann	Rangers (sub. M. Burchill)
D. Hutchison	Everton
J. Collins	Everton

Result 1-0 Hutchison

SCOTLAND INTERNATIONAL LINE-UPS AND STATISTICS 2000-2001

29th March 2000
v FRANCE *Hampden Park*

N. Sullivan	Wimbledon
P. Telfer	Coventry City (sub. A. Johnston)
C. Davidson	Blackburn Rovers
C. Dailly	Blackburn Rovers
E. Hendry	Coventry City
P. Ritchie	Hearts (sub. S. Pressley)
W. Dodds	Rangers
B. Ferguson	Rangers
K. Gallacher	Newcastle Utd. (sub. M. Burchill)
D. Hutchison	Everton
C. Cameron	Hearts (sub. N. McCann)

Result 0-2

2nd September 2000
v LATVIA (WCQ) *Riga*

N. Sullivan	Tottenham Hotspur
D. Weir	Everton (sub. Naysmith)
C. Dailly	West Ham United
M. Elliott	Leicester City
E. Hendry	Coventry City
C. Davidson	Leicester City (sub. C. Cameron)
T. Boyd	Celtic
B. Ferguson	Rangers
W. Dodds	Rangers (sub. Holt)
D. Hutchison	Sunderland
N. McCann	Rangers

Result 0-1 McCann

7th October 2000
v SAN MARINO (WCQ) *Serravalle*

Sullivan	Tottenham Hotspur
McNamara	Celtic
Naysmith	Everton
Elliott	Leicester City
Hendry	Coventry City
Dailly	West Ham United (sub. Weir 36)
Dodds	Rangers
Cameron	Heart of Midlothian
Gallacher	Newcastle United (sub. Dickov 65)
Hutchison	Sunderland
McCann	Rangers (sub. Johnston 46)

Result 2-0 Elliott, Hutchison

11th October 2000
v CROATIA (WCQ) *Zagreb*

Sullivan	Tottenham Hotspur
Weir	Everton
Naysmith	Everton
Elliott	Leicester City
Hendry	Coventry City
Boyd	Celtic
Johnston	Rangers (sub. Dickov 46 (sub. Holt 89))
Burley	Derby County
Gallacher	Newcastle United
Hutchison	Sunderland
Cameron	Heart of Midlothian

Result 1-1 Gallacher

15th November 2000
v AUSTRALIA *Hampden Park*

Gould	Celtic
Weir	Everton (sub. Elliott 46)
Boyd	Celtic
Dailly	West Ham United
O'Neil	Hibernian (sub. Hendry 51)
Ferguson	Rangers
Dodds	Rangers
Burley	Derby County (sub. Dickov 63)
Cameron	Hearts (sub. McCann 46)
Hutchison	Sunderland
Matteo	Leeds United

Result 0-2

24th March 2001
v BELGIUM (WCQ) *Hampden Park*

Sullivan	Wimbledon
Weir	Everton
Boyd	Celtic
Lambert	Celtic
Hendry	Coventry City
Elliott	Leicester City
Ferguson	Rangers
Burley	Derby County
Dodds	Rangers (sub. Gallacher 88)
Hutchison	Sunderland
Matteo	Leeds United

Result 2-2 Dodds 2 (1 pen)

SCOTLAND INTERNATIONAL LINE-UPS AND STATISTICS 2001-2002

28th March 2001
v SAN MARINO (WCQ) *Hampden Park*

Sullivan	Wimbledon
Weir	Everton
Johnston	Rangers
Lambert	Celtic
Hendry	Coventry City
Elliott	Leicester City (sub. Boyd)
Cameron	Hearts (sub. Gemmill 82)
Burley	Derby County
Dodds	Rangers
Hutchison	Sunderland
Matteo	Leeds United (sub. Gallacher)

Result 4-0 Hendry 2, Dodds, Cameron

25th April 2001
v POLAND *Bydgoszcz*

Sullivan	Wimbledon
Nicholson	Dunfermline Athletic
Davidson	Leicester City (sub. Weir 72)
Boyd	Celtic
Dailly	West Ham United
O'Neil	Hibernian (sub. Gemmill 73)
C. Miller	Dundee United (sub. Caldwell)
Rae	Dundee
Dodds	Rangers (sub. Crawford)
Cameron	Hearts (sub. McClaren 46)
Booth	Twente Enschede (sub K. Miller 80)

Result 1-1 Booth (pen)

1st September 2001
v CROATIA (WCQ) *Hampden Park*

Sullivan	Tottenham Hotspur
Weir	Everton
Naysmith	Everton (sub. Gemmill 84)
Lambert	Celtic
Elliott	Leicester City
Matteo	Leeds United
Dailly	West Ham United
Burley	Derby County
Booth	Twente Enschede (sub. Dodds 71)
Hutchison	Sunderland
McCann	Rangers (sub. Cameron 51)

Result 0-0

5th September 2001
v BELGIUM (WCQ) *Brussels*

Sullivan	Tottenham Hotspur
Weir	Everton (sub. Cameron 74)
Naysmith	Everton
Lambert	Celtic
Elliott	Leicester City
Matteo	Leeds United
Dailly	West Ham United
Burley	Derby County (sub. McNamara 82)
Dodds	Rangers
Hutchison	Sunderland
Boyd	Celtic (sub. Booth 57)

Result 0-2

6th October 2001
v LATVIA (WCQ) *Hampden Park*

Sullivan	Tottenham Hotspur
Weir	Everton
Davidson	Leicester City
Dailly	West Ham United
Elliott	Leicester City (sub. Rae 71)
Cameron	Wolverhampton Wanderers
Nicholson	Dunfermline Ath. (sub. Booth 62)
Burley	Derby County
Freedman	Crystal Palace
Hutchison	Sunderland (sub. Severin 76)
McCann	Rangers

Result 2-1 Freedman, Weir

16th May 2002
v SOUTH KOREA *Busan*

Sullivan	Tottenham Hotspur
Dailly	West Ham United
Weir	Everton
Ross	Rangers
Caldwell	Newcastle United
G. Alexander	Preston N.E. (sub. Stockdale 62)
Gemmill	Everton
Stewart	Manchester Utd. (sub. Severin 46)
Johnston	Middlesbrough (sub. Kyle 65)
Dobie	West Bromwich Albion
O'Connor	Hibernian (sub. Williams 46)

Result 1-4 Dobie

SCOTLAND INTERNATIONAL LINE-UPS AND STATISTICS 2002

20th May 2002
v SOUTH AFRICA *Hong Kong*

Douglas	Celtic
Stockdale	Middlesbrough (sub. Alexander 69)
Caldwell	Newcastle United (sub. Wilkie 46)
Dailly	West Ham United
Weir	Everton
Ross	Rangers
Gemmill	Everton (sub. Stewart 86)
Williams	Nottingham Forest (sub Severin 78)
Dobie	West Bromwich Albion
Kyle	Sunderland
Johnston	Middlesbrough (sub McFadden 62)

Result 0-2

21st August 2002
v DENMARK   *Hampden Park*

Douglas	Celtic
Ross	Rangers
Weir	Everton (sub. Severin 78)
Dailly	West Ham United
Stockdale	Middlesbro' (sub. Alexander 72)
Ferguson	Rangers
Lambert	Celtic (sub. McInnes 81)
McNaughton	Aberdeen (sub. Crainey 46)
Naysmith	Everton (sub. Johnston 73)
Kyle Kevin	Sunderland
Thompson	Rangers (sub. Dobie 56)

Result 0-1

7th September 2002
v FAROE ISLANDS (ECQ) *Toftir*

Douglas	Celtic
Ross	Rangers (sub. Alexander 75)
Crainey	Celtic
Dailly	West Ham United
Weir	Everton
Ferguson	Rangers
Dickov	Leicester City (sub. Crawford 46)
Dobie	West Brom. (sub. Thompson 83)
Kyle	Sunderland
Lambert	Celtic
Johnston	Middlesbrough

Result 2-2   Lambert, Ferguson

12th October 2002
v ICELAND (ECQ)   *Reykjavik*

Douglas	Celtic
Ross	Rangers
Wilkie	Dundee
Pressley	Heart of Midlothian
Dailly	West Ham United
Ferguson	Rangers
McNamara	Celtic (sub. Davidson 34)
Crawford	Dunfermline Athletic
Thompson	Rangers (sub. Severin 85)
Lambert	Celtic
Naysmith	Everton (sub. Anderson 89)

Result 2-0   Dailly 6, Naysmith 63

15th October 2002
v CANADA   *Edinburgh*

P. Gallacher	Dundee United
Dailly	West Ham United
Pressley	Heart of Midlothian
Wilkie	Dundee (sub. Murray 75)
Anderson	Aberdeen
Alexander	Preston North End
Gemmill	Everton (sub. Severin 66)
Devlin	Birmingham City
Ross	Rangers (sub. Davidson 45)
Crawford	Dunfermline Athletic (sub. Kyle 89)
Thompson	Rangers (sub. McFadden 81)

Result 3-1   Crawford 2, Thompson

20th November 2002
v PORTUGAL   *Braga*

Douglas	Celtic
Anderson	Aberdeen (sub. McInnes 24)
Pressley	Heart of Midlothian
Wilkie	Dundee (sub. Severin 83)
Alexander	Preston North End
Lambert	Celtic (sub. Williams 78)
Dailly	West Ham United
Naysmith	Everton
Ross	Rangers (sub. Devlin 46)
Dobie	West Brom. Albion (sub. Kyle 78)
Crawford	Dunfermline Athletic

Result 0-2

93

SCOTLAND INTERNATIONAL LINE-UPS AND STATISTICS 2003

12th February 2003
v EIRE *Hampden Park*

Sullivan	Tottenham H. (sub. Gallacher 45)
Caldwell	Newcastle United
Anderson	Aberdeen
Dailly	West Ham United
Alexander	Preston North End
Lambert	Celtic (sub. Gemmill 45)
Ferguson	Rangers (sub. Cameron 65)
Naysmith	Everton
McCann	Rangers (sub. Smith 65)
Crawford	Dunfermline (sub. Thompson 65)
Hutchison	West Ham United (sub. Devlin 45)

Result 0-2

29th March 2003
v ICELAND (ECQ) *Hampden Park*

Douglas	Celtic
Wilkie	Dundee
Pressley	Heart of Midlothian
Dailly	West Ham United
Alexander	Preston North End
Ferguson	Rangers
Lambert	Celtic
Hutchison	West Ham United (sub. Devlin 82)
Naysmith	Everton
Miller	Wolves (sub. McNamara 82)
Crawford	Dunfermline Athletic

Result 2-1   Miller, Wilkie

2nd April 2003
v LITHUANIA (ECQ) *Kaunas*

P. Gallacher	Dundee United
Pressley	Heart of Midlothian
Dailly	West Ham United
Wilkie	Dundee
Alexander	Preston North End
Lambert	Celtic
McNamara	Celtic (sub. Gray 78)
Naysmith	Everton
Hutchison	West Ham Utd. (sub. Cameron 85)
Miller	Wolverhampton Wanderers
Crawford	Dunfermline Ath. (sub. Devlin 57)

Result 0-1

30th April 2003
v AUSTRIA *Hampden Park*

P. Gallacher	Dundee United
Wilkie	Dundee
Webster	Heart of Midlothian
Pressley	Heart of Midlothian
Devlin	Birmingham City (sub. Smith 84)
Burley	Derby County (sub. Cameron 64)
Dailly	West Ham Utd. (sub. Gemmill 45)
Hutchison	West Ham United (sub. Miller 62)
Naysmith	Everton
Thompson	Rangers (sub. Crawford 45)
McFadden	Motherwell

Result 0-2

27th May 2003
v NEW ZEALAND *Edinburgh*

Douglas	Celtic
Ross	Rangers (sub. Alexander 45)
Naysmith	Everton
Webster	Heart of Midlothian
Pressley	Heart of Midlothian
Dailly	West Ham United
Devlin	Birmingham City
McNamara	Celtic (sub. Kerr 82)
Kyle	Sunderland (sub. Gray 59)
Crawford	Dunfermline Athletic
McFadden	Motherwell

Result 1-1   Crawford

7th June 2003
v GERMANY (ECQ) *Hampden Park*

Douglas	Celtic
Ross	Rangers (sub. McNamara 74)
Pressley	Heart of Midlothian
Webster	Heart of Midlothian
Naysmith	Everton
Devlin	Birmingham City (sub. Rae 60)
Lambert	Celtic
Cameron	Wolverhampton Wanderers
Dailly	West Ham United
Crawford	Dunfermline Athletic
Miller	Wolves (sub. Thompson 90)

Result 1-1   Miller

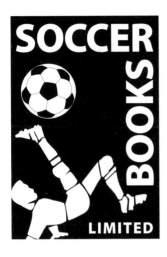

SOCCER BOOKS LIMITED
72 ST. PETERS AVENUE (Dept. SBL)
CLEETHORPES
N.E. LINCOLNSHIRE
DN35 8HU
ENGLAND
Tel. 01472 696226   Fax 01472 698546
Web site http://www.soccer-books.co.uk
e-mail info@soccer-books.co.uk

Established in 1982, Soccer Books Limited has the biggest range of English-Language soccer books and videos available. We are now expanding our stocks even further to include many more titles including German, French, Spanish and Italian-language books.

With over 100,000 satisfied customers already, we supply books to virtually every country in the world but have maintained the friendliness and accessibility associated with a small family-run business. The range of titles we sell includes:

YEARBOOKS – All major yearbooks including Rothmans (many editions), Calcios (many editions), Supporters' Guides, Playfair Annuals, North & Latin American Guides (all editions), African Guides, Non-League Directories.

CLUB HISTORIES – Complete Statistical Records, Official Histories, 25 Year Records, Definitive Histories plus many more.

WORLD FOOTBALL – World Cup books, International Line-up & Statistics Series, European Championships History, International Statistical Histories and much more.

BIOGRAPHIES & WHO'S WHOS – of Managers and Players plus Who's Whos etc.

ENCYCLOPEDIAS & GENERAL TITLES – Books on Stadia, Hooligan studies, Histories and dozens of others.

VIDEOS & DVDS – Season's highlights, histories, big games, World Cup, player profiles, F.A. Cup Finals with many more titles becoming available all the time.

For a current printed listing of a range of our titles, please contact us using the information at the top of the page.

Our web site offers a secure ordering system for credit card holders and lists our range of 1,000 new books, hundreds of videos and an ever increasing number of DVDs.

Supporters' Guides & Other Titles

This top-selling series has been published annually since 1982 and contains 2002/2003 Season's results and tables, Directions, Photographs, Phone numbers, Parking information, Admission details, Disabled information and much more.

THE SUPPORTERS' GUIDE TO PREMIER & FOOTBALL LEAGUE CLUBS 2004

The 20th edition featuring all Premiership and Football League clubs. *Price £6.99*

THE SUPPORTERS' GUIDE TO NON-LEAGUE FOOTBALL 2004

The 11th edition featuring all Conference, Unibond Premier, Rymans Premier and Dr. Martens Premier clubs. *Price £6.99*

THE SUPPORTERS' GUIDE TO WELSH FOOTBALL 2004

The 4th edition featuring all League of Wales, Cymru Alliance & Welsh Football League Clubs + results, tables & much more. *Price £6.99*

THE SUPPORTERS' GUIDE TO FOOTBALL PROGRAMMES 2004

Produced in conjunction with *Programme Monthly* magazine, this book contains an appraisal of the programmes of all 92 Premier and Football League Clubs during the 2002/2003 Season. *Price £6.99*

FOOTBALL LEAGUE TABLES 1888-2003

The 6th edition contains every Football League, Premier League, Scottish League and Scottish Premier League Final Table from 1888-2003 together with Cup Final information. *Price £9.99*

NON-LEAGUE FOOTBALL TABLES 1889-2003

The 2nd edition contains final tables for the Connference, it's 3 feeder Leagues and the 4 North Western Leagues in England (which were not included in the 1st edition). *Price £9.95*

These books are available UK & Surface post free from –

Soccer Books Limited (Dept. SBL)
72 St. Peter's Avenue
Cleethorpes
N.E. Lincolnshire
DN35 8HU